Mighty Men of Valor

Becoming the Men We Need to Be

Also By True Horizon Publishing

NONFICTION

Marriage Rocks!: Some Assembly Required

The Childless Factor: By Choice or Design

Mighty Men of Valor: Becoming The Men We Need to Be

First Edition

Artwork Designed by Michael Sullivan
Edited by Robert Williams

ISBN: 978-0-9818396-1-5

10 9 8 7 6 5 4 3 2 1

Dedications

To my Dad, Willard (Shorty) Montgomery, who was not perfect but made a valiant effort.

To Charles Olson who taught me that my walk should always be in concert with my talk.

To Mark DeMatteo who taught me the value of having an impact.

To Pastor Ben Sanders who showed me that there is more to life than just existing.

To my wife, Lisa, who every day challenges me to be the Mighty Man of Valor I need to be. She is the best shieldmaiden any warrior could ask for.

Acknowledgements

Graphics Design/Cover Art – Ms. Sarah Sullivan, who along with her Dad, Michael turned an idea into a reality.

Editor – Robert Williams, who tried to tell me he would be completely candid and was true to his word.

THE WORLD NEEDS MEN...

who cannot be bought;
whose word is their bond;
who put character above wealth;
who possess opinions and a will;
who are larger than their vocations;
who do not hesitate to take chances;
who will not lose their individuality in a crowd;
who will be as honest in small things as in great things;
who will make no compromise with wrong;
whose ambitions are not confined to their own selfish desires;
who will not say they "do it because everybody else does it";
who are true to their friends through good report and evil report, in
adversity as well as in prosperity;
who do not believe that shrewdness, cunning, and hardheadedness are the
best qualities for winning success;
who are not ashamed or afraid to stand for the truth when it is unpopular;
who can say "no" with emphasis, although all the rest of the
world says "yes."

Charles Swindoll

Living Above the Level of Mediocrity

P.107-8.

Contents

Chapter 1 - What is a Mighty Man of Valor? 7

Chapter 2 – A Mighty Man Has Character……………………………...14

Chapter 3 – A Mighty Man Believes in the Cause……………………24

Chapter 4 – Mighty Men are known by Their Actions………………37

Chapter 5 – Mighty Men are known by Their Attitudes……………..52

Chapter 6 – Mighty Men Build and Protect Their Thoughts………..66

Chapter 7 – Mighty Men Build and Define Their Lives……………....82

Chapter 8 – Mighty Men are Righteous…………………………………88

Chapter 9 – Mighty Men are Mentors………………………………......95

Chapter 10 – Mighty Men are Made, Not Born……………………..104

Chapter 11 – Mighty Men Live By a Code…………………………….112

Chapter 12 – Mighty Men Are Men of Faith………………………....118

Chapter 13 – Mighty Men are Disciplined…………………………...127

Chapter 14 - Mighty Men Are Persistent……………………………..138

Chapter 15 - Mighty Men Have No Fear …………………………….146

Chapters 16 – Mighty Men are Consistent ………………………….156

Chapter 17 – Lessons from the Field…………………………………165

Conclusion…………………………………………...171

Introduction

When I was teenager I read anything and everything Conan the Barbarian. I remember as a youth, working on the farm in the summer, my job was to move the irrigation lines twice daily. These were quarter-mile long mechanisms with wheels every twenty feet or so and a motor in the middle which turned the whole line; each shift of the 1300 foot-long pipe was a very slow process – slow enough for a teenage boy to steal a page or two of his favorite comic book or novel.

Conan was a bad dude! He was big; he was muscular; he was good looking; he could fight his way out of any situation and the ladies showered him with affections. He lived in a world where you were either strong or you were dead and a man made a name for himself solely with his wits or his skills as a warrior. Conan was born on a battlefield and matured quickly, by age fifteen he was already a respected warrior who had taken part in many battles. After one such glorious battle he was struck by wanderlust and began the adventure of a lifetime during which he encountered skulking monsters, evil wizards, tavern wenches, and beautiful princesses. He roamed throughout the ancient kingdom nations as a thief, outlaw, mercenary and pirate. As he grew older, and news of his daring exploits spread, people whose respect he had won gathered around him, allowing him to realize his ambition to command larger and larger units of men. In his forties, he seized the crown of Aquilonia, the most powerful kingdom of his time, thus becoming the greatest king the ancient world had ever known.

I wanted to be just like Conan. I knew he was a fictional character, but it didn't matter, the dream burned within me. I wanted to travel the world fighting bad guys with nothing but my wits and my sword and if fortune smiled on me one day, I might become king just like Conan. It never really occurred to me that I was a young boy living in a small town in southern Idaho and there weren't too many kingdoms up for grabs. The only 'sword' I had to practice with was whatever piece of lumber I could find laying around my Dad's shop and my shield of choice was usually the lid from my parents trash can. The only 'monsters' I encountered were usually my friends and after a while they got tired of being chased by a crazy kid with a stick and a trash can lid. Likewise, the 'maidens' I knew at the time weren't too hip on the idea of lavishing me with their favors; most of the time they ran away screaming. I used to think sometimes that the only way I would get to be like Conan was to go looking for trouble which would then give me a reason to conquer something. Don't get me wrong, I wasn't a problem child who was always in trouble; I'm just telling you how I thought and felt.

Even today I sometimes have dreams where I am a hugely muscular barbarian fighting off hordes of enemy soldiers and eventually obtaining the prize – whatever it might be. A treasure of jewels, a kingdom of land, or the love of beautiful women, the prize didn't really matter to Conan. He was all about the fight itself and how well he performed in it; to him the prize was not as important as acquitting himself against all challenges and odds. He didn't care what other people thought of him but rather spent the early years honing his fighting skills taking in any and every discipline that was available. At the time, Conan was the only "mighty man of valor" I knew and he epitomized the very ideals I held true in my young heart.

What happened to the days when we as men looked forward to battle and the glory of victory? When did we stop caring who won or lost just so we ourselves didn't have to get involved? When did we decide that it was not worth our time and energy to right the wrongs we see in our world? When did we stop wanting to be Superman and settled for being Clark Kent? Where along the line did we stop attempting to set the example for that which we know is correct? When did we stop being like the Mighty Men of Valor that God so passionately describes throughout the Old Testament? Where are the descendants of these men? Has their example of manhood been forgotten? Was their example not enough? Today, most of us men are a far cry from the Biblical standards of old. There was a time when we would be drawn to the sounds of conflict as opposed to having the din send us running in the opposite direction. There was a time when we as men would rather stand for our beliefs than crouch in abject fear when called to defend them. There was even a time in the not-so-distant past when we thrived and were thrilled at the prospect of conflict.

Whether it is a physical battle, a financial struggle, a diplomatic confrontation, or a political skirmish, we as the Mighty Men of our families and nation need to rise up and start shouldering the responsibilities given to us by our God, our communities, and our country. We must heed the call that has gone out from our spiritual Commander-in-Chief and begin to prepare for the strife that is before us and that will come. That call has gone out each and every day since the beginning of existence itself. It is a call for heroes. It is a need for warriors. We must learn to wear our armor and how to use the weapons provided to us. Learning the techniques necessary to face life's challenges might come in handy as well. In short, we must learn to become the up-in-front, in-your-face leaders that are so needed in today's world. .

This book is intended as a call to men but there is something for women here, too. First, you as a woman probably have quite a few misconceptions of what a man should be. You have these misconceptions because you either have no examples in your life to compare to or you have decided that real men just do not exist so why go searching for them. You think they are a myth and you will just have to settle for the best of a bad lot. Ladies, there are men out there right now who want nothing more than to place you upon a pedestal and care for you unceasingly but they are afraid. They are afraid that they will not be that man. They have not yet made the choice to be who they need to be or who they want to be. Some of you know that these mighty men exist but are unsure why they do not present themselves or where they may be found. The causes of all these feelings will be discussed in the chapters to come.

Secondly, I would submit to you that as you mature in life, you will want to learn what to look for in your future "soul mate." Your knight in shining armor is out there; you just have to be patient that God will help you find him. The only way to accomplish this is to know what you're looking for.

Third, many of you may entertain the thought of becoming a mother someday, and you will play a critical role in teaching your sons themselves to be Mighty Men of Valor.

We have all heard the old stereotype about men never wanting to stop and ask for directions. That's probably truer than we'd like to admit, but it isn't just men who are guilty. The world is full of both men and women, all driving full steam ahead, who never want to stop or even slow down to ask for guidance. When a woman takes time to learn about and understand a man's role in life, she also gains insight into her own role. Throughout history, there are stories of women taking their places alongside men on the field of battle. Ancient Norse sagas refer to 'shield maidens', whose role was to support the men as they held the line in battle; perhaps giving rise to the old saw that behind every great man is an even greater woman.

God intends for all of us to take our place in the battles before us whether they be spiritual, political, financial, or moral battles but it is the man's role to lead the fight and the women that we as men are to be defending and protecting have their place in the fight as well. I think to some degree women understand a man's need to be man more than we as men do ourselves. But we as men understand more than anyone our need to stand up for that which we know is right and just, to throw ourselves in harm's way, if you will. We need to throw ourselves in danger's path once in a while, if for no other reason than to feel the thrill of victory and accomplishment. If we as men don't feel challenged from time to time, and know that something great has come from our efforts, we begin to wonder and question our purpose. We need to start growing backbones and become like the Mighty Men of old – ready to hazard our lives for country, king and cause. We need to suit up, mount up, and begin to fortify ourselves for the coming fight. We as men need to begin taking responsibility for our own lives and for those who have been trusted to our care. There are castles that need defending, wives that need protecting, and children that need to be raised in a manner such that they learn to become mighty themselves.

No amount of success at the office or any other place in the world can compensate for our failures at home if we choose not to join the battle. When all the battles are fought and our time here is done, if we do what is expected of us, if we do what *needs* to be done, we shall know that our Lord and Savior counted us as Mighty Men of God and that is ultimately the only title or praise any of us as men need.

To some lesser or greater degree, we all want to take the path of least resistance, to float along like a leaf in life's stream; it's the path of least resistance, and following it minimizes exposure to danger. . But this is not and never was God's plan for Mighty Men. We were designed to live life to the fullest. To just exist from day to day, avoiding the battle or pretending that it has nothing to do with you is more dangerous and painful than joining the fight. People are relying on us and to be seen as an unreliable person is worse than being seen as a coward. The Bible talks much about mighty men of valor who had character and integrity, it says that many of them demonstrated excellence in various areas and because of this excellence rose to positions of great leadership. This is what God wants for you today. He wants you to take your rightful place in your home, in your community, and in your nation. He wants you to step forward and carry his banner as your own and live by the same code of conduct that His mighty men lived by. We all do exactly what we decide to do; we are the sum of our decisions and if we as men do not stand up and become the influencers of our generation now we will lose all that we hold dear. So let's begin and begin now!

Chapter 1
What is a Mighty Man of Valor?

"Just as a diamond requires three properties for its formation – carbon, heat, and pressure – successful leaders require the interaction of three properties – character, knowledge and application. Like carbon to the diamond, character is the basic quality of the leader…but as carbon alone does not create a diamond; neither can character alone create a leader. The diamond needs heat. Man needs knowledge and study and preparation….the third party, pressure – acting in conjunction with the carbon and heat – forms the diamond. Similarly, ones character, attended by knowledge, blooms through application to produce the leader" – General Edward C. Meyer, Former Army Chief of Staff

Our modern world has done a beautiful job of feminizing men. Just look at the commercials we see on TV these days. Here is the typical scenario: The wise, rational wife tries to convince her brainless, weak-willed husband that this way and that way is the correct course of action. Throughout the commercial or sitcom, the viewer has to bear with the idiot husband as the wife shows the obviously better way (usually whatever the purpose of the commercial is). They may seem funny or cute when they make the man look either inept or incompetent but by doing so they portray them as less than men and also lessen the impact men are supposed to have on those around them. Men, according today's media, are weak, dim-witted, silly to the point of indecisiveness, and express humiliating and embarrassing feminine sensitivities. Boys are taught early in life that to be outwardly combative or overly aggressive will lead to social isolation and unpopularity. Society as a whole trains them to prepare for peace, but not for what they will confront in the real world or what may be necessary to achieve that peace. They are teased, taunted, and humiliated for their "emotional limitations." The media portrays them as emotionally clumsy and inept, making them even more resentful and confused about what was expected of them. They are billed as not willing to face reality and therefore lack control over their emotions and desires, presenting the image that they are spineless puddles of goo. They are

6

portrayed as individuals more willing to change businesses, children, or even wives than change themselves. Sadly, many men recognize how they are perceived and, either consciously or not, begin to emulate in their lives what they see as society's expectations for them. They are no longer the champions they so desperately want to be and are ridiculed for even attempting to become one.

As men we are sometimes called upon to perform deeds we see as within the context of what one would call 'mighty' and we are also called to take care of what we see as petty. Whether it is stepping on a nasty spider, or checking out the weird sounds coming from downstairs at night, maybe you're confronting a habitually sinful friend or a chronically late employee. It could be an entire armored division on some distant plain of battle or something as simple as shoveling snow from your elderly neighbor's walkway or helping a stranded mother with children to change a flat tire. In any case, you are the defender, protector, warrior and soldier of your realm. Mighty Men are the personification of might and power as well as courage. They are the living examples of what God intends a warrior to be. They are men given to the service of others. They live, eat, think and breathe duty, honor, courage and might. They are sometimes referred to as "men of the in-between," meaning they stand in-between their families, their community, and their nations to protect from any who would hurt, harm, or destroy.

In the Book of Second Samuel, one single verse stands out as the ultimate statement of what the warrior ethos should be. In verse 12 of chapter 10, it states;

> *"Be of good courage, and let us play the men for our people, and for the cities of our God: and the LORD do that which seemeth him good."*

Men stand tallest when they are doing what they were designed too. We must not only "play" the man but we must"be" the man. Mighty Men move us by igniting our passions and inspiring us to be something better than we are. A Mighty Man does not just perform impossible deeds but also possesses high moral standards; he has principles that he lives by and stands for. True examples of manhood can still be found in the world today, but sadly they are few and far between. Most people's only resource for discovering real manhood is what they can glean from books or movies. To most, these are the only places where representations of "honor" and "character" still exist. An interesting social development took place near the start of the 20th century as children began to look towards their mothers for guidance more than their fathers. When they are born the first person a baby sees is a nurse, usually female, then as they are raised they become accustomed to a dominant female presence, whether in the home or day care. When they go to school or Sunday school they are taught by female teachers. In some cases, they even see a female leading the congregation, so it's no wonder that our children grow up with little concept of male leadership – they simply have not been exposed to it. Our children find more of the traits of a mighty man in their video games than they do in their fathers. Wives have turned to soap operas for their knights because their husbands are not the men they once were. Our communities are lead by males who perform the tasks necessary because it benefits them personally. You as a man need to strive to become the very best you can be if for no other reason than your family and friends deserve nothing less.

When we Christians read the Bible, we tend to skim over lists of names and genealogies thinking they are unimportant. But God has included them in his Word for a purpose, and one thing it shows us is that God is interested in individuals. The Old Testament tells us that there were between thirty and thirty-seven Mighty Men under David's command; considering the rareness of the breed, that great of a number indicates that there is always room for Mighty Men in God's army. It will take commitment, dedication, strength, obedience, and hard work on our part, but the opportunity is always there. God can never have too many Mighty Men of Valor.

The Bible tells us *who* the Mighty Men were, but more importantly *what* they were. What makes a man stand out among his peers? What makes him noteworthy? What is it about some men that allow them to stand out in a crowd? Did you know that one can be "mighty" in a negative sense? In the Old Testament, the righteous intermarried with the wicked and the results were mighty men, not in stature, but in wickedness. Their every thought was an evil one and there were those who held these men in high regard. They were so good at being bad that God cleansed the earth with a year-long flood.

They were the warriors and military leaders of the ancient world. They were the core; the very best and brightest the world had to offer. They knew they were meant to live, not just exist; to soar and not grovel. They thrived on taking risks and relished a good challenge in much the same way one looks forward to a good meal. Though frequently outnumbered in battle they were consistently victorious. They were a different band of warriors and a different breed of men because they thought and acted as such. They were different in ways that set them apart from mainstream society. They were called "Mighty" because their deeds were great but also because their character and sense of honor allowed them to stand out in a crowd. They were the literal "Band of Brothers" but they weren't always that way.

Before David became king, he spent some time on the run; he was having a string of bad luck and was running for his life. King Saul wasn't happy with his performance at work and so had driven him out of the palace. At one point, David even had to pretend to be insane just to protect himself while in the enemy camp. It had all come to a head when he found himself hiding in a cave with a bunch of other misfits in the same predicament. The Bible tells us there was no one else like them in the world and that they were unmatched in battle skills. They were an unruly group of malcontents and they were greatly in debt to everyone around them. They were tired, dirty, hungry, and a bit impatient. It looked like David was surrounded with a group of losers and he was their chief. However, these men had one redeeming quality that they shared; they believed in David as he followed God, which allowed them to become his mighty men of valor. David may have had problems but he was good at attracting people to his banner and cause. Because of his leadership and the qualities they carried with them, this bunch of malcontents and losers eventually were forged into the core of a mighty and disciplined force that did what no Israelite army had ever been able to do in overcoming one of the greatest enemies their nation had ever known. They were fugitives who became heroes; they were the merry men of the Old Testament and their leader was the first Robin Hood. They didn't just appear on the scene as shining examples of all that was known as good and righteous but they did become something more than they were. They were transformed from something that was loathed, and at times looked upon with disdain, into winners and over-comers.

They did some amazing things like killing eight hundred armed men in single combat with nothing more than spears. Three of this select group once fought their way through the entire Philistine army with no other thought on their minds than to obtain a cup of water for their king. One Mighty Man, Eleazar, once stood alone to deny the enemy a barley field and fought an entire army, which eventually fled in fear. On a cold wintry day, one Mighty Man jumped into a pit with a lion for the purpose of killing it with his bare hands. One convinced an entire race of people that they could conquer a city by marching around it for a week and then blowing a few horns to make the walls crumble. The Bible mentions a "Special Forces" group that fought with King David from the tribe of Gad who were experts with sword and shield. They were "as fierce as lions and as swift as gazelle in the mountains." The Bible says that the weakest of these men could take on a hundred regular troops and the strongest challenged a thousand.

Some of the Mighty Men mentioned were not warriors in the purest sense. While most were trained for war, some apparently had the knack for military intelligence. They were spies and plied their craft with all the stealth and precision required. We read of these men and we see real life superheroes fighting for their King, their Country and all the values they held dear. We see men who believed in the cause, their leader, and did what was asked of them no matter the consequences, because to do otherwise would have been unthinkable. We listen as they talk about living up to something, some elusive, ethereal cause, hoping to be worthy of it. These men were the stuff of legends. Just once I'd like to see Hollywood come up with something that comes close to the deeds of these Mighty Men.

In today's world, many of us will get the opportunity to stand on the field of battle and perform mighty deeds of physical strength or military daring, but for the most of us we have only to defend the driveway and pick up the kid's toys. We will not get to be William Wallace in Braveheart nor King Leonidas in 300. We will not experience the fear, excitement, and apprehension as we don our suits of armor, buckle on our swords or slam home another magazine when the battle looms before us. We will never get to see the "elephant" as today's combat veterans describe it. We may never feel the rush of adrenaline as we hold the shield wall against thousands of blood-thirsty enemies who would have us die. Society would have us believe that most men today wouldn't even want to be put in that kind of situation, risking our very lives for nothing more than an ideal or cause. They say we are spineless wonders with no more substance than that of jellyfish whose purpose is to provide comic relief to those who wish to hide their own inadequacies. We are seen as inconsequential factors who have no purpose except to sometimes perform menial tasks.

The turning point in our lives will come when we stop seeking the male the world wants and start being the man we need to be. It has been said that the gates of manhood are guarded by the demons of our souls, and those demons are different for each man. The true test of manhood is to discover what those demons are, and then to conquer them. This is the only way one who desires to be a man may pass through the gates. Most men have at least one demon in common; they are not sure if they are the man they need to be. They harbor doubts as to their effectiveness and influence on the world around them. They don't know if they have what it takes when the enemy stands before their gates.

You cannot know who you are or what you are capable of until you face some adversity. You cannot know the strength of the heart until it is under pressure and you cannot know what kind of man you are until you look hardship and pain in the eye, face it, and choose to either run from it or overcome it. We will never find out if we deserve the rewards if we are not willing to face the risks. We will never know the answers until we are willing to face the questions themselves. Every aspect of our lives will want us to take the easy road and there will be times when we would agree but we also know in our hearts we shall never know what would have been if we choose not to listen to that small voice that tells us to continue forward and turn our face away from safety.

I have to believe, though, that there are still men out there who hear the call in their hearts, and relish the opportunity to run toward the sounds of conflict, ready to raise the standard for their families and their country. But there needs to be more of us holding that line. The wall is thinning and at some point there are even gaps. There needs to be more men willing to step up and make themselves known as true defenders of this world. This same world thinks we are like sheep who do nothing but stand around helplessly and need nothing but basic sustenance. They think we will not fight or are always looking for the easy way out. They think that we will turn and run at the first sign of trouble and not stop until we are sure we are out of danger. We are described as defeated even before we enter the ring. We as men need to change that perspective; to do that we must change our perspective of ourselves first.

So what is a Mighty Man of Valor? Who are they and how do you become one? Do you even have what it takes? They are men whose very actions and attitudes differentiate them from the crowd. They are men who espouse certain traits and ideals that when put out for all to see stand head and shoulders above the rest. They are that one particular individual that always stands out in a group not because of the way they look but because of the way they speak. So what are these traits and ideals? I have compiled a list of certain attributes that I believe will answer these questions and all men should either exemplify now or be in the process of developing in themselves. I am in no way a perfect example of any of the traits, but, like you, I am always working to improve and develop them in myself. It is in no way inclusive of all the attributes necessary but it is a good place to start. These values or attributes will shape your character and these choices, decisions, and actions will become the framework of your character.

Chapter 2
A Mighty Man Has Character

"Character is the firm foundation stone upon which one must build to win respect. Just as no worthy building can be erected on a weak foundation, so no lasting reputation worthy of respect can be built on a weak character." - R. C. Samsel

It all begins here.

For one to be a Mighty Man of Valor one must have impeccable, unimpeachable, character. Character development is the foundation of any successful enterprise, whether building a company or teaching someone how to be a man, it has to start here. Character is one of those things that is hard for most people to describe but I am a simple guy so I try to keep things just that way, simple. Character, to me, is making the decision to do the right thing no matter what. It's that easy. You demonstrate character through your behavior and actions. People can teach what they know but they reproduce what they are. To put it another way, who you are determines how you act. British psychologist William McDougall once said, *"Will is character in action."* Willpower is the source of your action and, therefore, the source of our character. When we will to do good, and do so, we have good character, but when we will to bad things or neglect our responsibilities, we have bad character.

Character is a set of behavior traits that define what sort of person you are. It determines whether a person will be forthright in dealing with others and will obey the laws and rules placed upon them. Character should not be confused with personality; it is not the same thing. Personality is a dynamic set of characteristics possessed by a person that uniquely influences his or her motivations while character consists of learned behavior. No one is born with good character yet everyone, regardless of background, enters the world with the opportunity to become a person of exemplary character. Personality may vary with the situation or circumstance but one's character should be always the same. Character is not the same as reputation; character is what you are and reputation is what people say you are. Character is the embodiment of self-discipline and the will to be a person who displays that trait. Some call it the 'Warrior

Ethos' which derives from the unique principles by which every person lives. At its core, character is grounded in a refusal to accept behavior that is lacking and is developed through discipline and commitment. It is what motivates warriors to fight for one another. They develop a mindset that they would rather die than leave their comrades behind or let them down. It is the characteristic that businessmen look for before stepping into a new venture with someone. They want someone whose private life mirrors their public life and vice versa. It is what makes us better sons, brothers, fathers and husbands. It is what we look to instill in ourselves as we live our lives. The warrior ethos requires determination to do what is right and to do it with pride.

Most decisions come down to making a choice between two paths; character or compromise. All of us are given the opportunity to make these kinds of decisions every day. Which path we choose with our decisions determines the course of our character. When people complain about their lives or circumstances, they often blame others for their unhappy state of affairs. If it isn't the fault of others, then they claim it is due to "bad luck" or how "unfair" the world is. They seem to blame everyone and everything except themselves. The complainers have also chosen a path, it is a path that diverts attention from possible solutions to their problems, but it is a path nonetheless. Character development is a life-long process; it will not happen in an instant. Some of the choices you encounter may not be awe-inspiring but they are character-building decisions nonetheless. It may be as complex as what to do with some damaging information you have discovered about a competitor, or it may be as simple as whether or not to take your neighbor's copy of the Wall Street Journal from their driveway.

Lisa and I once had this great couple who lived next door to us and they had a daily subscription to the Wall Street Journal. Now, the Journal is one of the few newspapers I will take the time to read. I don't subscribe to it myself only because I am one of those high-tech fellows who would rather save the money and read it online. Anyway, one day I was out in the driveway and I noticed that there were at least three copies of the paper laying in their driveway. Vaguely, I remembered that they had said something about being out of town for a week or so the last time I spoke to them so I started thinking to myself...by the time they get them they will be really old news, so they most likely would not miss an issue or two. Certainly if I took just one copy, they wouldn't notice, or suspect me of taking it if they did. You may be thinking the same way I did. No one's going to know and no one's going to care. You may be right about the not caring part but you are completely wrong about no one not knowing. You see, I knew. I knew that no matter how innocent I wanted it to be and no matter how I justified it, it was still stealing and it was wrong. You see, you must become a Mighty Man on the inside long before you will be recognized as one on the outside. To this day I am in a small way proud to say that my neighbor's newspaper is safe.

"Our character is what we do when we think no one is looking" - *Karl Otto Von Schonhausen Bismarck*

How a person deals with the challenges in his life determines how his character develops. If you consistently make bad choices, you will consistently be known as someone without character. If you make good choices, your character will be revealed. Every time you make the right choice you become stronger and every time you make the wrong choice you become weaker. If you do nothing then you will achieve nothing. Here is a basic truth: As a man, you serve as the caretaker of your family's morals. You must, therefore, promote the highest standards of ethical conduct with your every act. People of character consistently act according to principles – not just what might work for the moment. They make their principles known and consistently act in accordance with them. So what must you as a Mighty Man know about character?

Talk Will Not Develop Your Character
Anyone can say that they have character but actions are the true indicator. Your character determines who you are, and who you are will determine how you act. You can never, or should never, separate the two from each other. If your actions are not lining up with your character then you need to take a good hard look at your character and find out why. Make yourself your #1 project. Make a point of developing good habits and you will learn to make good decisions. The decisions you make will determine the actions you take, which in turn will determine the results you achieve. Men of character say what they mean but, more importantly, do what they say. It doesn't matter what you promise; all that matters is that you do

what's been promised. If you say you're going to take the trash out, then make sure it gets done. If you promise a client his product will be done by a certain date, then do everything in your power to make sure he gets it. If you make an appointment, keep it! I once read a statistic that 80% of appointments are never kept or are late. It's so bad now that many doctor's offices call a day in advance to remind people of their appointments. Let's say you promised to take the kids camping next weekend; don't schedule something else just because it may be more important to you. It may seem inconsequential to you, but it is an opportunity to set a standard; your kids are watching and will absorb your lesson about how seriously they should take their commitments. A great place to start is with promises you make to yourself. If you tell yourself you're going to perform a certain task then do it! Stop standing around talking about it! A man is defined by the quality of his action, not his words. A good rule of thumb is to always under promise and over perform.

Character is a Choice
There are many choices in life that you don't get a say in. You don't get to choose who your parents are, nor do you get to choose how they raised you, some say you don't get to choose your IQ. You get to choose your character, though. You create it every time you make choices, bit by bit, little by little, day by day. You get to choose to run or stay and fight. You get to choose to bend the truth or shoulder the weight of it. You get to choose to take the easy way out or pay the price. As you live your life the choices you make will forge your character. Hold yourself to a higher standard than is required even if it means standing up to those closest to you. Every failure in life can be traced back to a compromise of character. Don't allow yourself to compromise your integrity, instead be resilient and always do what is right.

Somewhere near a battlefield over 200 years ago, a man in civilian clothes rode past a small group of exhausted battle-weary soldiers digging an obviously important defensive position. The section leader, making no effort to help, was shouting orders, threatening punishment if the work was not completed within the hour. "Why are you are not helping?" asked the stranger on horseback. "I am in charge. The men do as I tell them," said the section leader, adding, "Help them yourself if you feel strongly about it." To the section leader's surprise the stranger dismounted and helped the men until the job was finished. Before leaving the stranger congratulated the men for their work, and approached the puzzled section leader. "You should notify top command next time your rank prevents you from supporting your men - and I will provide a more permanent solution," said the stranger. Up close, the section leader now recognized General George Washington, and also the lesson he'd just been taught.

One cannot be sure that the story is true but it is an excellent example of two individuals' character. One with questionable character who thought position was more important than those he lead, and one who placed the people and their welfare before his own needs. It was not the moment that defined these two individuals' character but rather their response to the moment that made clear the difference between them. Only one of them realized that his character was a choice, not a chance, and it was also not a thing to be waited for. The section leader believed he deserved respect by virtue of his rank, while General Washington knew that respect is not awarded, appointed, or assigned, but must be earned every single day.

When Oscar Wilde arrived for a visit to the US in 1882, he was asked by customs officials if he had anything to declare. He replied: "Only my genius." Fifteen years later, alone and broken in prison, he reflected on his life of waste and excess. "I have been a spendthrift of my genius...I forgot that every little action of the common day makes or unmakes character."

A person's character can be described two ways; as a thermostat or a thermometer. If their character is like a thermostat they change the temperature of the environment around them by displaying exemplary character. They raise or lower the temperature by raising or lowering their standards. If a person's character is like a thermometer, they reflect the temperature of their environment. They let their character be defined by the people and situations they are faced with. Today, ask yourself; was I a thermostat or a thermometer?

You will always be limited by Your Character
If you do not have a bedrock foundation for your character your entire mission will eventually fold like a house of cards in a stiff breeze when the challenges come. Your organization will recognize it and will not follow you and worst of all, eventually, you will know it. This will lead you to

periods of self denial, depression, and inevitable failure. If you find yourself headed down this road, stop whatever it is you're doing right now and seek help. Don't sit there and think that this is just a valley you're in and that it will eventually pass. Do not fool yourself by thinking that throwing money at the problem will solve it. Ignored cracks in any foundation will eventually become more destructive in time. Your character cannot withstand the cracks placed upon it by dishonesty. Every time you are dishonest, you weaken the strength and effectiveness of your character. Ask yourself, do my actions match my words? Do I follow-through on promises I make? Can people count on me to uphold my end of the bargain, even if I think it's bad one? When people shake my hand do they know that my word is my bond or do they think they just shook hands with a dead wet fish? Your character will always accentuate the content of your message.

"A leader not only stays above the line between right and wrong, he stays well clear of the 'gray areas' as well" – John Maxwell

One of the better known examples of character I know is from the Old Testament and is a story about a guy named Uriah. The Bible lists Uriah as a Mighty Man due, in my opinion, to his actions when no one was looking. You see, Uriah was an officer in King David's army and while he was out campaigning with the army, David and Uriah's wife Bathsheba began an adulterous relationship. David should have been out with his army setting the example and leading his men but instead he was home lounging around and relaxing. It was a recipe for disaster from the beginning. As a result of she and David's relationship, Bathsheba became pregnant. David tried to cover up the problem by calling Uriah home from the battlefield on the pretense of requiring information from him about the state of the war. David's plan was to accept Uriah's "report" from the front lines, and then give him leave to spend time with his family. Contact between the couple could have hidden the adulterous nature of her pregnancy by David. Uriah, though, was reluctant to leave his comrades-in-arms on the battlefield, and when he finally did come to report to King David, he refused to extend his time away from the battlefield for a visit with his wife.

David ordered. Uriah refused. In today's terms it would be viewed as an order that could not be carried out in good conscience. In fact, he went so far as to declare to his king that there was no way he was going to follow that particular order. Uriah refused to follow the order because his personal code of honor, his character, would not allow him to leave the battle. He knew that honor was a matter of living the values of respect, duty, loyalty, integrity and courage in everything he did. His fellow warriors were still out on the battlefield living in tents, eating military fare, and preparing themselves for the upcoming conflict. It was common at the time for warriors preparing for battle to abstain from sex, as a practice of discipline. Uriah considered it the ultimate insult to his ideals, his friends, and their sacrifice if he were to be back home safe and sound enjoying the company and comforts of his family.

After repeatedly refusing to see his wife, Bathsheba, David sent him back to the battlefield with a private letter ordering the commanding general of his army, Joab, to put Uriah up on the front lines and have the soldiers move away from him so that he would be killed. Joab ordered Uriah and a small group of soldiers to attack where the greatest force of the besieged was congregated, acting as a kind of forlorn hope. In the days of muzzle-loading muskets, a forlorn hope usually referred to the first wave of soldiers attacking a breach in defenses during a siege. It was a great way to get promoted but usually ended with most members killed or wounded. The intent was that some would survive long enough to seize a foothold that could be reinforced, or at least that a second wave with better prospects could be sent in while the defenders were reloading or engaged in mopping up the remnants of the first wave.

A fight took place in which Uriah and the officers with him advanced as far as the gate of the city, where they were finally shot down by the archers on the wall. Although Uriah may have lost his life, he never sacrificed his principles and now his example of excellent character is known throughout history.

Character such as Uriah's can only be obtained if three conditions are in place:

A solid foundation

Almost every failure in life can be attributed to a compromise of personal integrity. How many of us will admit to shoplifting or stealing at some point in our lives? How many times have we lied or cheated? How many times have we said to ourselves "I am happy with my level of character?" The greatest need in our society today is someone who will demonstrate exceptional character. Many choose to build their lives on a foundation of compromise, only to discover that when the chips are down and their character is needed the most, they cannot withstand or overcome the assailing pressures. Without strong character everything you or I attempt to achieve will crumble and fall. We must build our lives on principle rather than theory. Theoretical character will not stand well against a very real challenge. Mighty Men of Valor don't negotiate their principles because situations or people alter. They do not compromise the standards by which they live their lives. We all would like to know that we walk this path supported by those around us, but unfortunately sometimes this will mean walking alone. Others may not see the value of a solidly built foundation of character as we do but they will recognize its difference from the norm.

A strong heart

I recently read a story about an actor with a career spanning over half a century in which he told of his humble beginnings and the character choices that impacted his life immeasurably. "I was newly married and a new father. We were barely making it; living off my waiting tables and doing a few acting jobs here and there. A man called one day offering an assignment paying a lot of money (back then) to play a young rebellious man spewing out obscenities to his father. After thinking of the disrespect it would bring to my father, a good man, I turned it down and declared I would only play roles in which my family could be proud. Almost a month later, the man called back with a respectable role and an offer to represent me as my agent. He said he could not stop thinking about me. He said, 'If a man feeding his family off pennies could turn down an assignment offering this much money, there had to be something to him.' He represented me as my agent for 30 years until his death. The role he offered me was 'Guess Who's Coming to Dinner?'" That actor was Sidney Poitier, who went on to win the Oscar for Best Actor for his role in Lilies of the Field in 1963. Mr. Poitier's choice during that difficult time changed the course of his life but it was a choice that could not have been made without a strong heart.

The heart must be capable of conquering the unpleasant dictates of discipline as well as laziness, disobedience, and unproductive desire. These qualities inhibit progress, and hearts that cannot overcome them will always be defeated and conquered. As with any challenge in life, the day of that challenge is not the time to begin preparing. We must decide in our hearts what our convictions are and resolve to remain firm in them. And we must do it now, before the problems come calling. This knowledge and firmness of conviction will be confirmed in our actions and manifested in our attitude. A strong heart is the result of decisions made in the moments of choice which define who you are and what you are about.

An ability to ascertain the truth of matters
This enables a person to put the truth in its rightful position. It allows you to see the difference between right and wrong or, as it used to be described, "distinguishing between glass and real diamonds". Sun Tzu once said; *"If you know the enemy and you know yourself, you need not fear the result of a hundred battles. If you know yourself but not the enemy, for every victory gained you will also suffer a defeat. If you know neither the enemy nor yourself, you will succumb in every battle."* A Mighty Man of Valor must know the truth in himself before he is able to ascertain the truth of any given situation. He must be able to recognize the difference between his character and his reputation. I once had a friend ask me what that difference was. I think William Hersey Davis can answer it best for us.

The circumstances amid which you live determine your reputation; the truth you believe determines your character.
Reputation is what you are supposed to be; character is what you are.
Reputation is the photograph; character is the face.
Reputation comes over one from without; character grows up from within.
Reputation is what you have when you come to a new community; character is what you have when you go away.

Your reputation is learned in an hour; your character does not come
to light for a year.
Reputation is made in a moment; character is built in a lifetime.
Reputation grows like a mushroom; character grows like the oak.
A single newspaper report gives you your reputation; a life of toil
gives you your character.
Reputation makes you rich or makes you poor; character makes you
happy or makes you miserable.
Reputation is what men say about you on your tombstone;
character is what angels say about you before the throne of God.

A man who seeks to improve his reputation will be confused by the man of character. He tends to assume that all men have the same motivations and attempts to manipulate others with those incentives. His arguments are often shallow and when he cannot convince others with reasonable discussion he attempts to intimidate with threats. He tends to be shocked when his childish attempts at persuasion are ignored by someone who has already examined his own heart and not the opinion polls. A man who seeks to increase his reputation has a habit of pointing to his degrees and awards and suggest that you respect his opinions because they in turn have been respected by influential men in high places. Men of character point at the Bible and suggest that all opinions should be weighed on God's scales, not society's.

As a Mighty Man of Valor, character needs to be exercised in all areas of your life – big and small. Character is defined through your actions and therefore defines who you are. How you act should be of concern to you no matter where you or who you are around. Character is not something that you turn on and off depending on whose presence you are in. Always remember that the highest reward for a person's character is not what they get from it but who they become because of it. Once the road to superior character development has been chosen one can begin to determine what the mission is.

Chapter 3
A Mighty Man Believes in the Cause

"Far better it is to dare mighty things than to live in the gray twilight that knows not victory nor defeat" - Theodore Roosevelt

Beliefs are convictions we hold as true. They affect our attitudes, our actions, and our reactions to setbacks and successes. They are influenced by our experiences, upbringing, culture, heritage, and traditions. Beliefs matter because it is through them that we make sense of our experiences. They provide the foundation for our personal values, which shape our behavior and therefore our mission. To be a Mighty Man of Valor, you must know what your mission is and believe in that mission. The Mighty Man must always have an end to which he is headed. In life, as in football or soccer, none of it means anything unless he knows where the goal posts are. You must understand and hold dear the cause or purpose for which you strive. To do anything less negates any effort put forth to accomplish the tasks set before you. When you believe in your mission you assume an offensive posture; you become actively engaged in accomplishing whatever tasks are necessary to accomplish your goals. Have you ever noticed that when someone challenges your beliefs you automatically assume a defensive posture in order to defend your position? If you do not truly believe in the cause, you can find yourself hemmed in behind a defensive perimeter, and rarely has a battle ever been won while on defense.

In ancient times, when an enemy attacked, people would retreat and hunker down in whatever fortification was handy at the time, such as a castle or a fort. Their hope was that they might be able to wait out the attacking enemy. The problem with this tactic was that the defenders had limited resources inside the castle but the enemy had almost unlimited resources at their disposal. Food and water would only last so long before the defenders realized they would have to go on the offensive to break the siege.

When we are challenged, sometimes we tend to react as though we are under siege, we to sit around inside our castles hoping someday something will happen to relieve us. We hole up and peek over the walls once in a while in the hope that one time when we look, the challenge may just be gone. Mighty Men don't operate this way. They don't hunker down or back up or retreat to safety. They are bold and go on the attack because they are aware that if they don't they run the risk of starving mentally, economically, and spiritually. Our commitment to our beliefs works the same way. If we withdraw somewhere hoping that we can accomplish the mission without actually getting involved, or support the cause by letting events tend to themselves, we risk losing the intensity of our motivation because we are not actively engaged in the process. We are, quite literally, afraid of the outcome because we don't believe in ourselves enough. If we go on the attack, using our belief as the catalyst, we accomplish more and conquer more without the threat of losing our commitment because our convictions are too strong to let us give up.

People don't know what they don't know. They refuse to believe in things even in the face of evidence. There are people, even today, who still believe the Moon landings in 1968 were a hoax, the Holocaust never happened, their cell phones spew enough radiation to cook popcorn, Bill Gates will send them money if they forward enough email and that Elvis is still alive working at a convenience store in Cleveland despite all the evidence to the contrary. Look at how many people refuse to believe the Bible and all that it contains, even though science and archeology regularly confirm what it says. Take, for instance, Noah's Flood. Many either believe the Flood was a made-up fantasy to scare people or that it was only a *local* flood, confined to somewhere around Mesopotamia. Talk to any geologist and they will tell you that at some point in Earth's past the entire world was covered by water. They can prove that by analyzing the geological record anywhere on the planet. On the subject of the local flood, only a few questions are necessary to prove even the most hardened doubter wrong. If the Flood was local, why did Noah have to build an Ark? He could have walked to the other side of the mountains and missed it. If the Flood was local, why did Noah gather up all of the animals? There would have been other animals to reproduce that kind if these particular ones had died. If the Flood was local, how could the waters rise to 25 feet above the mountains? Water seeks its own level. It couldn't rise to cover the local mountains while leaving the rest of the world untouched. Yet there are people, even Christians, who still doubt the Flood. It doesn't matter how much evidence one produces to the contrary, people will not believe something they don't want to believe. Belief is a choice.

How many times have we heard or read about how Roger Bannister was the first person to run a mile in less than four minutes? As a lifelong runner, in superb physical condition, Roger Bannister certainly had the ability to break the four minute barrier, but what most people do not realize is that Roger Bannister first had to *believe* that he could do it. You see, Bannister's beliefs dictated his actions, which in turn dictated his results. After the devastation of his failure at the 1952 Olympics, (he came in fourth) Bannister spent two months deciding whether to give up running. But instead, because he was a Mighty Man at heart, he didn't give up and decided on a new goal: To be the first man to run a mile in under four minutes. He believed he could do it. Accordingly, he intensified his training and did hard intervals every day. As a medical student at St Mary's Hospital, Paddington, Bannister chose to use his lunch hour for a nine minute jog to Paddington track, where he ran 10 x 400m in about 60 seconds with two minutes rest, then he ran back to work. The whole procedure took 46 minutes, leaving him 14 minutes to eat his lunch. On May 6th, 1954, Roger Bannister became the first human being to run a mile in less than four minutes and because of his willingness to overcome his own doubts and show the world it could be done, within one year, 37 runners broke the belief barrier. The year after that, 300 other runners did the same thing.

In the Old Testament, Nehemiah is doing his job as the cup-bearer for Artaxerxes one day when he hears some terribly disturbing news from home. He heard of the run-down and desperate condition of Jerusalem, and became depressed. For many days he fasted and mourned and prayed for a solution or remedy to the problem. After some time the king observed his condition and asked the reason for it. Nehemiah explained the challenge to the king, imploring his permission to go and rebuild the walls of Jerusalem. Nehemiah was amazed when the king consented. In fact, not only did he consent, but he also sent Nehemiah on his way fully equipped with supplies, purchase orders for more supplies, and royal letters for safe passage.

Nehemiah didn't exactly get the red-carpet treatment when he arrived, but he charged forward nonetheless. He immediately surveyed the damage, declared his intent to rebuild the walls, and began assigning the different areas of responsibility. Nehemiah surveyed the city secretly at night, and formed a plan for its restoration; a plan which he carried out with great skill and energy, so that the whole wall was completed over an astounding 52-day span. Neighboring leaders were hostile, and taunted him incessantly. This went on until they eventually realized that the Jews were serious about renovating the walls, at which point they presented some serious opposition in an attempt to stop the rebuilding. However, Nehemiah planned ahead for just such a contingency, and the people were ready, taking turns standing watch on the wall and carrying weapons while they work, even as the building continued.

As adventuresome as this story is in detailing the daring and courage of the people, I think the important point is that Nehemiah *believed* in the mission no matter what challenge was presented to him. No matter what happened, nothing stopped him from completing the wall! From the very moment that the purpose was placed in his heart, he moved forward, never letting anyone or anything deter him from completing his mission. Only someone with an overwhelming, all-encompassing belief and commitment to see things through to completion can overcome overwhelming, all-encompassing problems.

If you want your family or your organization to be committed to whatever mission or assignment you have embarked upon then you yourself had better be committed first. It all starts with and eventually ends with you. You, as a Mighty Man of Valor, must set the example first and set it best. In so doing, those around you will evaluate and duplicate that commitment and then they will become committed. But remember, you must first be worthy of their commitment. If your commitment is lackluster don't be surprised if the people who follow you seem less than enthusiastic about the cause. The level of personal commitment that you have in any endeavor will determine how much investment those that you serve will put into it. Effectively demonstrating commitment to your mission, whether it be to the organization's principles or to yourself, is never easy. Demonstrating commitment is hard but worthwhile work. Wavering commitment is usually seen as no commitment at all and the only way to achieve a reputation for commitment is through determination and persistence. Genuine commitment will always stand the test of time.

In high school, I had a friend who owned a 1977 Chevy Nova which was his pride and joy. He had bought it and rebuilt it so that it was quite literally a street-legal race car. One day, in the course of conversation, he told me that he had decided to take the engine apart and install a new racing camshaft in an effort to get more horsepower from the car. I had seen him do other kinds of work on the car like body repair and brakes and such but never anything as complicated as a partial engine rebuild. I told him unequivocally that he might as well call the local shop to do it because without knowing what he was doing it would take him forever to complete if he could even manage it at all. I knew as soon as I opened my mouth that I had hurt him on some deep level but it didn't stop him from moving ahead with the project anyway. He knew he could perform the task and nothing I said or did was going to dissuade him from it.

A week later I went over to his house to see what he was doing and he and his car were in the driveway. Parts of his engine were on the front lawn and out in the street. I have to be honest, I was still amazed that he was even attempting such a complicated operation and told him so...again. He moved his head from under the hood, looked me right in the eye and told me that if I wasn't going to help then I might as well go home because he didn't have time for people who were not committed. He didn't have time for people who didn't believe. Needless to say, a whack with a baseball bat might have done less damage but I realized I did deserve the hit. I knew right then and there that he was serious and that he was going to do it now matter what. We stared at each other for a few moments and then I handed him a wrench and asked if there was anything else I could do to help. I am proud to say that because of his perseverance and tenacity he had the fastest car in the county and he even let me drive it once or twice.

By first establishing a purpose and a sense of mission, you will be much further along the path of completion and those elements will help guide your decisions and determine the best course of action. So what is a cause? During the 80's and 90's it used to be the "right" thing for an organization to develop a mission statement. Mission statements are great for galvanizing the corporate entity, but we as men need to go further than that. A mission statement is a declaration designed to inform the members of the organization what exactly the purpose and intention of that organization is. In my opinion there is a huge difference between a mission statement and a cause, in much the same way that there is a huge difference between a battle cry and shouting at the enemy. No one ever steps into an uncomfortable or dangerous situation for a mission statement, but for a worthy cause we will move Heaven and Earth. To a Mighty Man of Valor, a cause is something that stirs your blood. It is a call that burns hot within you and pushes you far beyond your limits of endurance. It may even keep you up late at night. For something you truly believe in you will go farther, do more, and risk everything. A cause is one thing that you will not give up on or give in to no matter the circumstances. It may cause you an enormous amount of pain before it is all over, but, if the cause is truly worthy, the effort getting to the finish line will seem like a walk in the park once it is over. It is something that you believe in so strongly that nothing short of death itself could dissuade you from it.

Belief in a cause allows you to expect the best, prepare for the worst, and celebrate it all in the end. When we face challenges that lie just beyond our ability to deal with mentally, physically, or spiritually, we enter into the realm of faith and hope. We must enter this realm willingly because as we face these new frontiers in our lives we will truly discover what we were meant to do. They are like mountains that many of us attempt to ignore but sooner or later they become so prominent that they cannot be disregarded. We realize that we cannot go over them or move around them. It is these same mountains that we as Mighty Men must face and conquer; because only by overcoming them do we learn to teach others to face their own mountains. Nehemiah faced these same mountains when he began the rebuilding of the wall and he also knew that if he himself didn't show commitment then the people would not show theirs. My friend with the car knew that no one would believe in his ability to rebuild the engine in his car unless he believed first.

So how does one develop and establish their beliefs?

Stop and Recognize Your Ability to Believe.
I believe each of us is born with a predisposition to value ourselves as someone with inherent worth regardless of conventional definitions of success, failure, or the opinions of others. There is no other more powerful directing force in human behavior than belief, and it begins with our belief

29

in ourselves. Your beliefs have the power to create and to destroy but you must first recognize that power within you. A belief starts in your mind and delivers a direct command to your nervous system which in turn directs your muscles to perform whatever task is set before them. Now, your muscles may not be capable of performing said task but your mind (your belief) doesn't know that. We create beliefs to anchor our understanding of the world around us, and thus, once we have formed a belief, we will tend to continue with that belief. Most rational people believe that air exists but how do we know that as truth? We know because we can see the physical evidence of air around us. We can feel it when we breathe and we see the effect of it when the wind blows. We tend to never question our beliefs because we know them to be true. I have no doubt in my mind as to the existence and purpose of air. I know I can believe in air because I know the effect it has on the world around me.

I have a friend who once held the belief that it was cool to complain and criticize. After he had alienated his friends, the circumstances caused him to identify, question, and change this belief about what is cool and attractive to others. He realized that he had the ability to change his beliefs. This was not an easy task for him and it also initially caused a certain amount of pain but he was serious about turning his life around. The alternative was even worse than what was required to change. He, like Nehemiah, had to stop believing that this was all there was to his life and start believing that there was something more for him to do.

Stop the Wishful Thinking.
Wishful thinking is interpreting facts, reports, events, perceptions, etc., according to what one would like to be the case rather than according to the actual evidence. It also may be defined as a formation of beliefs and decisions according to what might be pleasing or imagined instead of by appealing to evidence or reason. The desire to believe is a real and powerful drive that can carry you either into genuine impact or dangerous fantasies and delusions based on what you wish is true. Instead of just believing whatever you want to believe, get serious about discovering the truth of what it is you were meant to do. Some atheists argue that much of theology, particularly arguments for the existence of God, are based on wishful thinking because it takes the desired outcome (that there is a God) and tries to prove it through reasoning which can be wished "true" in the

mind of the believer. Some theologians argue that it is actually atheism which is the product of wishful thinking, in that atheists may not want to believe in any gods or may not want there to be any gods. As much as I want to, there isn't much chance I will ever qualify for the astronaut program, so it wouldn't do me much good to dwell on it. Don't get me wrong, I personally think anything is possible but there are times when we need to distinguish between possible and probable and move ahead with that which will best help us accomplish our mission. We as men must take possession of our own thoughts with conviction and pray for the discernment we need to explore our beliefs, trusting that God will reveal our purpose to us.

Start Dealing with Uncertainty and Doubts.

Expect to encounter uncertainty as you search for real faith. Instead of ignoring the uncertainty you feel, let it motivate you to explore your purpose in fresh ways. Be honest about your struggles and humble about what you already know so you can move toward an authentic belief. Don't be afraid to honestly face your doubts. If you let your doubts motivate you to ask questions, they will ultimately lead you closer to your purpose. Don't be afraid to ask sincere questions. Don't let your circumstances determine your destination. Stick to your guns and remember the goals you have set. Constantly remind yourself of the positive factors and beliefs that brought you to this point and never abandon them. Remember that you don't have to have all of life's questions figured out today. You just need to take whatever steps you can take, and as you do, you'll discover more.

Stop and Look Beyond Yourself.

I had a friend once tell me that if we look beyond our own needs we can never have or do enough. If we see stop focusing on our own struggles and begin seeing the struggles of others we can never accomplish enough. And if we can find a way to step outside our own circumstances and help someone else we may very well find the answers to our own questions. Nehemiah saw the benefit of looking beyond his own self. He had a cushy job, a room at the palace, and a half-way descent boss, but he saw the need beyond the walls of his own comfortable enclosure. He saw that there were those who did not have it as good as he did and believed he could do something about it. If you are depressed, it is most likely that you are not looking far enough beyond yourself. Make it your mission to do or say at least one nice thing every day. It doesn't have to be time-consuming, expensive, or difficult but it should be something you wouldn't normally do or haven't done in awhile. Go out of your way to tell someone how much you appreciate their friendship, or be more specific by praising a job well done. You may think someone who excels at something doesn't need to hear it, but that couldn't be further from the truth. It's a natural, human need to crave appreciation to some extent. Just be sure you are genuine when complimenting people or they won't value it or you.

I once heard a speaker tell the following story about the birth of her first child. It seems that while she was in the delivery room, racked by labor pains, for a brief moment she closed her eyes. The next voice she heard was the attending physician shouting "open your eyes!" She looked at the doctor incredulously, wondering just what his problem was. What he told her next was one of the most profound lessons on focus she had ever been taught. The doctor told her that when you close your eyes you focus on the pain but when your eyes are open your mind is focused on the sensory input surrounding you, meaning you feel the pain less intensely. If we have our eyes open we can see other people's pain and challenges but if our eyes are closed we see only our own.

One of the greatest heroes of Scripture is Elijah. He boldly confronted King Ahab and told him that it would not rain nor would dew fall until he said so unless the king and his queen, Jezebel, wised up and got their lives right. He saw all kinds of miracles such as God sending ravens and having a widow woman feed him during the famine. When he confronted and challenged the four hundred prophets of Baal on Mount Carmel, God sent fire down from Heaven to consume the sacrifice, the altar, and the water. However, when King Ahab told his wife, the wicked Queen Jezebel, about what Elijah had done to her prophets of Baal, she became furious and sent word that she would have him killed by the next day.

Poor Elijah responded by becoming depressed and suicidal. Later when God confronted him at the mouth of the cave he was hiding in, and asked him what he was doing there, Elijah launched into a whining session. The way that God treated Elijah's depression was to get him to look beyond himself. He got him to see the need of those around him; to become other-

32

people minded. He motivated Elijah to see the larger purpose. If you are depressed, it is most likely that you are not looking beyond yourself. Open your eyes and heart to those whose lives are worse off than yours. When you do that your problems will become smaller or nonexistent.

Start Changing Your Behavior and Transforming Yourself from the Inside Out

God wants to do much more in your life than just get you to conform to good moral behavior. He wants to transform your whole soul from the inside out so you'll grow to become more of the man He intends you to be. It is also our belief that determines just how much of our potential we will be able to tap into. To do this we must examine our beliefs in sometimes excruciating detail. For example, do you believe that you can excel in whatever you do? Do you believe you are bad at certain things? I once thought I was terrible in English, so much so that I failed English in the 9th grade but yet here I am writing a book. Just because I don't know an adjective from a conjunction doesn't mean I cannot put thoughts on paper. Do you believe that other people don't like you? Do you believe life is full of problems? What are your beliefs about other people? Can you discipline yourself enough to find value in even the hardest personality? I have a good friend who talks too much, which irritates me to no end. I am the type of person who has always believed that if you don't have anything good or of value to say then don't say anything at all. My friend doesn't subscribe to that theory. He will talk and talk and talk about subjects that have absolutely no bearing on the original conversation. Does that make him a bad person? Not in my opinion. He still is a great husband to his wife and an even greater father to his sons. He loves the Lord and has made more positive contributions to society than most people ever dream about. He talks too much because that is what he used to do in his former job as a Congressional lobbyist. He had to spend his entire day, week after week, constantly talking to people in order to get his views and those of his constituents across. Once I was able to find the positive attributes of his personality my belief changed. I still think he talks too much but now I value what he does have to say (most of the time).

A belief is nothing but the generalization of a past incident. If a dog bit you when you were a kid, you might believe all dogs to be dangerous. If you have ever fallen from a tree or some other tall structure then you may believe that you are afraid of heights. A study by the National Institute of Mental Health found that over 18% of Americans suffer from some type of phobia. Research has shown that most phobias arise from some external event. To change a particular behavior pattern, we must identify the beliefs associated with it. Change those beliefs and a new pattern is automatically created, but realize that change does not occur overnight. You didn't get where you are overnight, so don't expect to get anywhere else in that short period of time either.

Stop the Excuses

Most of us are guilty of having done something we shouldn't have, or of not doing something we should have. When we are questioned about our misconduct, do we accept responsibility and admit we are at fault? Sometimes we do but a lot of the time we don't. Instead, we make excuses. Many of us say we're going to make changes in our lives, but few of us actually commit to improving the quality of our lives. We stay in a job we don't like and in a relationship that is painful; we blame our circumstances on the "hand we've been dealt." Whether you're sick of your financial situation, your poor health, or destructive temper, you have the power to change those circumstances. You have the ability to create the life you want and deserve, but only if you are willing to stop making excuses. When we make excuses and repeat them often enough, they become a belief. The belief then literally becomes a self-fulfilling prophecy. In order to counteract this prophecy we must accept responsibility. Only then can we evaluate our actions and take corrective measures to find solutions to our problems.

Creating the life you want begins with a choice. You must choose to eliminate the excuses in your life. You can choose the desired reality instead of the current reality, and commit to doing whatever it takes in order to create it. It's that simple. Whatever excuses are keeping you from committing to your mission, admit them to God and pray for His help to overcome them. Don't hold back any longer. Be willing to act on your desire to believe, even if you still have doubt or unanswered questions. Trust God enough to move toward Him as much as you can, and expect Him to meet you there.

Start (and Keep) Growing

As your belief increases and deepens, keep your eyes open, your mind working, and your spirit alert for all the new things God wants to teach you every day. One of the most common statements I hear from people is "I haven't read a book since college" or "I swore that if I got out of college I would never study again." The challenge with those statements is that life is a learning experience and those experiences will determine our growth. We must always be ready and willing to learn something new. It may be that you know how to do something really well and volunteering your services can benefit someone else. Or you can take on a challenge in an area in which you have no knowledge or experience. Either scenario can become a learning experience. I have been a lifelong reader. I still have the first two novel length books my parents ever bought me. I have sometimes found myself reading four or five books at a time on various subjects of interest to me at the time. Reading allows your mind to expand beyond the confines of the physical realm and explore regions that you would never go to without a little imagination. Reading about both sides of an issue gives you the opportunity to either reaffirm or change your beliefs. Reading allows you to grow and dream and form goals; most people hold themselves back due to their poor or non-existent dreams.

A dream is nothing more than a fantasy without a clear and concise endpoint. You have to be able to see the end result in your mind first. Remember, your thoughts determine your life. I came across the following article sometime back and wanted to share it as an illustration as to how misguided a person's beliefs can be.

> *Forget what you learned in elementary school--the earth is flat as a pancake. All that stuff about the earth being round and the sun being the center of the universe is a big joke, insists C.K. Johnson, president of the International Flat Earth Research Society, a group that takes great pleasure in poking fun at "globites." The organization, backed by 1400 members from around the world...or rather, from across the plane, gets scads of mail from dedicated teachers and students who blast it as a group of kooks and charlatans. Maybe it is, but Johnson claims the society's largest single group of members is doctors. Then come lawyers and other professional people, like engineers and*

architects. The Flat Earthers dismiss modern science as a club for sun worshipers and write off the American and Russian space programs as multi-billion dollar hoaxes. "The moon walk was done in a Hollywood set. All faked," says Johnson, a former airplane mechanic. Furthermore, he and his followers insist the sun is not stationary and does not set. They figure it to be a gigantic spotlight, 32 miles across, that moves in an ellipse just 3000 miles above the center of the earth. The other stars are just a lot of tiny holes poked in a huge canopy covering this planet. Do Flat Earthers believe in anything? "We believe the Earth is flat. Everything else is pure conjecture," Johnson replies. - Campus Life, December, 1979, p. 15.

It is one thing to say you have beliefs but yet quite another to know *why* you believe. I once heard a story about a mother who came down hard on her children whenever they tossed their hats on a bed. Finally one of the children asked, "Why is keeping hats off our beds such a big deal?" The answer she gave was that her mother never allowed hats to be placed on beds. One day, when her mother was visiting, the children asked their grandmother, "Why did you make such a big deal about not allowing hats to be on beds?" The grandmother said she did not know what they were talking about. At that point the mother of the children jumped in the conversation and said, "Mother, you did make a big deal about hats on beds. I remember when some next door children came to play and we all tossed our hats on the bed; you had told us not to do that and when we did, you grounded me for a week." "Oh," the grandmother replied, "that was because those neighbors usually had lice in their hair."

As a Mighty Man of Valor you must always know *what* you believe but also always know *why* you believe. Whether it be in the area of theology or politics, don't fall into the trap of regurgitating the facts that you have heard someone else say. Do your own due diligence. Always think about what it is you believe. Sometimes we spend so much of our available time and energy doing the work, and we think we are working towards the accomplishment of the mission, when in reality we have lost sight of the goal. It's like the old picture of the men laying the transcontinental railroad. Day after day, week after week, their entire existence was focused on driving the next spike on the rail. Some never once raised their heads to see the horizon or where the line was headed. It's at these times when we need to put down the hammer, take a breath and refocus on our beliefs.

Chapter4
Mighty Men are known by Their Actions

STAND FIRM: for well you know that hardship and danger are the price of glory and that sweet is the savour of life of courage and of deathless renown beyond the grave. - Alexander the Great, July 326BCE – in India when the Macedonians refused to advance.

In 400 AD a humble monk, named Telemachus, was so appalled at the horrible spectacle of the Roman games that he jumped onto the floor of the Coliseum and rushed to put himself between two gladiators who were attempting to kill each other.

In his rough, belted cloak, Telemachus would have been recognized as a holy man. Yet the crowd heaped abuse upon him, pelting him with stones. He pleaded, "Forbear, forbear! In the name of Christ, forbear!" but he was ignored. Many thought he was a clown performing for their amusement. When his actions distracted one of the gladiators and nearly cost him his life, the gladiator stabbed him through the heart. He looked into the eyes of his killer and begged one last time "In the name of Christ, forbear."

The crowd suddenly fell silent. Seeing a holy man lose his life trying to prevent gladiators from taking life was not what they paid to see. The Coliseum emptied as the crowds left in shame and humiliation. And that was the last time the Coliseum was ever used for gladiatorial combat.

Telemachus was as great a warrior as any of the Biblical Mighty Men; his actions cost him his life, but saved the lives of countless others by ending one of the most brutal spectacles in history. His actions, compelled by his spirit, are a prime example of the traits of the Mighty Men we should always be striving to be.

Mighty Men were meant to say more, be more, and do more than any others. They are individuals who are defined by their actions as well as their attitudes. In the immortal words of the United States Army, we were meant to "be all that we can be." From the day you were born you were given a special purpose that will outshine and outlive all other responsibilities you may have. Through the course of our lives we are trained and outfitted to complete this one particular task. It may take an instant or it may take a lifetime but the challenge is figuring out what that task may be. To fulfill that purpose is the reason why something or someone is created. Fulfillment of your God-given purpose must be the main focus of your life. Discovering the reason for your birth will unlock the door to manifesting your potential. Take the light bulb, for instance; the purpose of a light bulb is to light up an area that is in the dark. The light bulb has the capability to be used in many ways to produce a result; but in the mind of the creator, if the light bulb is used in any way other than its original purpose, it is being underutilized. It is only being used properly when it is demonstrating its reason for being created, which is producing light. It is our responsibility as mighty men to be light in the dark places of people's lives.

Mighty Men study the lives of other Mighty Men. They read about them, they listen to them and they take every opportunity to associate with them whenever possible. When we study the lives of great men, we learn how to follow in their footsteps and attempt to duplicate their greatness. Their lives teach us the qualities necessary to be great and what actions are likely to have what reactions. So many people today are oblivious to how associating themselves with a particular person, group, or identity can determine how successful they are in life. We tend to adapt ourselves to the people surrounding us whether they are at the workplace or at home. We do this because we want to be accepted or because following the norms of our culture and environment is sometimes the easier path. The problem is that we become like those we hang around. If we hang around someone who thinks a particular way, eventually we find ourselves thinking that way as well. But what can produce a negative result can also produce a positive one. Only another Mighty Man can influence the future development of a Mighty Man.

Phyllis Therous wrote, *"Small boys learn to be large men in the presence of large men who care about small boys".* Through the teaching and experiences of others you will learn about strength, honor, duty, virtue, etc. and what challenges they had to overcome in order to become Mighty Men.

I once had a friend edify me to a group of people by saying that I was likely the most loyal friend he had because when he did something or changed something I was behind him 100% and never questioned him. While I appreciated his glowing assessment I would like to clarify something before anyone flies off the handle and accuses me of being a blind follower. The reason I have never questioned this individual's actions is because I have never found anything wrong with them. I know from experience he takes great pains to evaluate every decision and every change before announcing it or implementing it but even then I personally process it through a few of my own brain cells. I ask myself questions like, how will this affect me? What will it do to my organization? Will it move us forward or be a deterrent to our mission? Once I am sure that I understand the mindset behind the change then yes! I am behind it wholeheartedly. We all have someone we follow or who mentors us and we all need to get behind them and stay there unless there is a reason to do otherwise. So many people I meet question everything and everyone to such an extent that they literally put themselves into a state of self-imposed inaction. They are so busy thinking that they stop moving.

Baron De Rothschild was one of the richest men who ever lived. Legend has it that the Baron once posed before an artist as a beggar. While the artist, Ary Scheffer, was painting him, the financier sat before him in rags and tatters holding a tin cup. A friend of the artist entered, and the baron was so well disguised that he was not recognized. Thinking he was really a beggar, the visitor dropped a coin into the cup. Ten years later, the man who gave the coin to Rothschild received a letter containing a bank order for 10,000 francs and the following message:

> *"You one day gave a coin to Baron de Rothschild in the studio of Ary Scheffer. He has invested it and today sends you the capital which you entrusted to him, together with the compounded interest. A good action always brings good fortune. Signed, Baron de Rothschild."*

In the Old Testament, the Book of 2 Samuel to be exact, we read of a Mighty Man of Valor named Benaiah. This particular Mighty Man was a cut above the rest of his fellow Mighty Men due to his exemplary actions. Benaiah's father, Jehoiada, a mighty man himself, set the example first so that his son would have a standard to live by and to live up to. But Mighty Men are not defined by the occupations of their parents. They are developed by and through the example of their parents. My father was an auto mechanic, and quite a good one at that. People from three counties used to bring their automotive challenges to my father because he knew almost instantly what the problem might be and he was fair if it warranted any sort of compensation. Most of the time he did it for nothing. I don't know the first thing about what is under the hood of my car. I know the basic principles that allow it to operate but the minute details are beyond me. My father was a good man when it came to dealing with people, though, and through his example I would like to think I developed a few good qualities as well. Behavior is not genetic. Just because your parents made wrong choices does not mean that you have to follow in their footsteps. God made you to be an individual, with individual thoughts and therefore individual choices for your actions.

Benaiah was born in Kabzeel, a city in the extreme south of Judah, near Idumaea (or Edom). His people inhabited the Negev Desert and the Arabah valley of what is now the southern Dead Sea and adjacent Jordan. When we first meet Benaiah he is already holding a leadership position. The Bible describes him as *"over the Cherethites and over the Pelethites"* and while we are not sure just exactly who these groups of people were, we know that Benaiah had authority over them in some way.

In 2 Samuel 23, Benaiah has just come from a fight. Apparently, two very ferocious looking "lion-like" men from Moab had taken offense with Benaiah and had proceeded to confront him with their differences. Benaiah didn't like their attitude, so he killed them. We are not really sure of the circumstances behind this altercation but it reminds me of the old western films when a bad guy wanders into town and decides to muscle people around. These kinds of situations always require two elements; someone willing to take a stand and someone to take a stand against. Benaiah was willing to take the stand. He didn't back away or back down when the fight started. He ran towards sounds of conflict. He didn't say to himself "this isn't my fight" or "it doesn't affect me." These two Moabites intended harm to the Jewish people and Benaiah was willing to fill the gap with his courage. These were not two run-of-the-mill soldiers on a drunken spree but rather were top-of-the-line Moab warriors. They were the best that Moab had to offer and were playing for keeps, but so was Benaiah, and because of his willingness to take action he was counted among his king's most trusted advisors and eventually was promoted to the head of the entire army. For all we know, Benaiah may have been scared but we know he wasn't a coward. He knew the difference between being a man and a mouse wasn't whether he was scared but rather what he did while he was scared.

The second time we meet Benaiah he is going toe-to-toe with a lion, who has somehow got himself into a pit and to top it all, this is all taking place on a cold, snowy day. Now you have to admit that spending time in a pit with a lion on a snowy day doesn't rank real high on most people's list of things to experience in life but it sure would look impressive on your resume should you be trying to secure a position as the king's bodyguard, which is where Benaiah eventually ended up.

Some of you may be asking what's the big deal and what does it have to do with what we are talking about? I'll answer by asking another question; have you ever been to a sporting goods store and seen the stuffed animals? Some may be cute and even cuddly. Some may even look a bit dangerous but do any of them fire your blood? Do they invoke that burning sensation deep in your mind and heart where the need to overcome and conquer stem from? Do you look at the animals and say to yourself, "just once in my life I would like to meet the most ferocious animal on the planet and look him right in the eye so that he may know that when this day is over only one of us is walking out of here! " Of interest is how the lion got into the pit; it is still common practice today when hunting a lion to dig a pit, camouflage it somehow, and then have the lion chase you so that he falls into the pit (hopefully before he gets to you) and is trapped. What is interesting about this story is not the fact that the lion was in the pit but rather why Benaiah was in the pit. Scripture doesn't tell us what Benaiah was doing when he encountered the lion. We don't know what he was thinking, either, what we do know is what he did once he was there. Benaiah went into the pit and I'd like to point out here that he didn't wait for the lion to come out to him. The normal operating procedure would have been for Benaiah to stand at the edge of the pit and shoot arrows into the lion or throw spears into him but not Benaiah. You see, Benaiah was a "hands on" type of man. He didn't try to avoid the situation even though the odds were against him. He recognized that great rewards required great actions and sacrifices. He jumped into the pit so that he could deal with the problem first hand. I don't think the idea of delegating even crossed his mind. One cannot be sure what the reason for trapping the lion in the first place was but I like to think it was because he was most likely doing what lions do best…scaring people. Benaiah could have sat around and waited for the lion to try and steal some livestock or attack one of the villagers but that wasn't who he was. Benaiah didn't wait for the lion to come to him – he went out and confronted the lion on his own turf.

We as Mighty Men need to confront life's problems the same way. We need to be proactive not reactive. We need to stop waiting for the need to come to us but rather we need to go to the need. We need to stop waiting for life to throw challenges our way and dealing with them after the fact. In some literal sense we need to grab life by the throat and deal with it NOW! How many times have we heard of a couple getting a divorce and one spouse or the other is in a state of shock because they were not even aware that there was a problem? We need to start taking action, and by doing so, become aware of what is happening around us. Mighty Men to do not wait for the fight to come to them, they go to the fight. Most of us tend to avoid confrontation due to fear. The challenge with that course of action is that avoiding confrontation is a confidence drainer. Our fear can be reduced through knowledge, which in turn will breed confidence in us. There are many fears about confronting problems or other people such as, fear of being wrong, fear of hurting someone's feelings, and fear of being ostracized. Do any of these sound familiar?

I used to believe that if I confronted someone it meant there was going to be an argument or I would make the other person angry. Either way, I always assumed a fight was coming. So I would avoid confrontations all together because when I got into a fight usually someone got hurt. I didn't want to hurt anyone and what normally ended up happening was that I would get more and more resentful of that person and the anger would build up. I would resent the fact that I was fearful of confrontation and instead of taking it up with the other person I would get more and more resentful of myself. I would keep looking for that person to make another wrong move which I could pounce upon and would collect evidence to build my case until one day when I had enough I would explode, usually saying or doing things that I would later regret. The problem was that I usually exploded on the wrong person because to unload on the person in question was in itself a form of confrontation which, again, I was trying to avoid. Another pattern I developed was to not say anything to the other person and as time went on I would avoid them and eventually remove them from my life. Eventually the evil looks and indifferent attitude would drive even the most open-hearted from me. One day I realized that I was not dealing with the issue at hand, that I was not being responsible. I also learned that running away wasn't the answer either. Mighty Men do not run away. I realized a simple conversation could have changed the whole dynamic of the problem and that a few direct questions here and there may have diffused any potentially volatile situation. I remember I used to get so upset with myself for not speaking up and taking a stand. My self-confidence and self esteem always took a hit because I knew in my heart I wasn't being the man I knew I could be. We as Mighty Men do not have to live like this so let's learn how to effectively deal with confrontation.

One major misconception when it comes to confronting people is that it will turn into an argument and someone will get angry. It sometimes may end up that way, but that is an outcome that you can control or at least lessen the potential for. If someone is upsetting or bothering you, anger should never be the solution. One option you may try is to move towards them, not away. Your first inclination will be to move away from the confrontation or to ignore the other person. This will only make them more defensive. Always make an attempt to move toward a defensive person, not away. Moving away provides emotional distance for you to hide and confirms their suspicion that you will not listen. Once you have established a beachhead and they know that you are truly trying to understand, remember what Jesus said. "Bless those who curse you, pray for those who mistreat you" (Luke 6:28). Bless and affirm their positive attributes. Recognize that they believe their cause is right and just. The greatest mistake people make is to engage a defensive person on issues of disagreement. Arguing with someone who is defensive always ends up in frustration and confusion. In fact, the problem usually escalates as each side responds to the other's accusations. Attempt to find facts or methods where you agree in an attempt get them off the defensive. Once they know that you are not on the attack, speak to them directly about the problem. Keep it as simple as possible and get it out in the open. Never use email or voice mail to state what is important to the situation. Always do it face to face so that they may not only hear your words but see the sincerity on your face and in your eyes. Try thinking with your head and heart instead of your hands. No one has to lose for you to create a win-win situation.

Lisa and I once had a rental property and for the most part we were blessed with great renters. One month we had a challenge present itself when the renter called to say that he would not have the money this month because he had just bought a new car. Now I personally started to resolve this situation by letting my emotions loose on the warpath. I wanted to go over to the property, knock the door down, grab this in'duh'vidual by the hair and beat the rent out of him. Oh yes! My Christian sensibilities were in full swing that day! Lisa, being the cooler and more intuitive part of this operation, decided to take a much more productive course. We went over to the property, calmly knocked on the door and asked to speak with the tenant. She calmly and succinctly explained to the tenant that he had a legal and moral obligation to pay the rent when it was due and that any other expenses he may have taken on were not our responsibility. Furthermore, she explained to him that if we did not have the agreed upon amount on the appointed day then we would begin eviction proceedings. Amazingly, once the tenant knew we were serious and understood the dynamics of the problem he agreed and the rent was paid on time and in full. And all without beating the living daylights out of him!

The reason I acted the way I did was because I feared confronting him on a rational level. I was afraid that he might see my fear and play upon it, making me look stupid in front of my wife. I allowed my fear of not understanding the facts involved to dictate my actions. The lesson to be learned here is that you cannot control another person's feelings or reactions to you. People choose how they react and how they feel toward a situation. Lisa's solution followed a time-tested method of resolving conflict. She analyzed all the data and then weighed the options available. She then chose the option that would most likely benefit all parties and then relayed the solution to the renter in a calm but firm tone.

Being assertive and confronting someone can be done with ease if you use a bit of common sense and the proper communication techniques. When you simply stick to the facts, not letting your emotions run rampant, and address what has happened and why it does not work for you it takes the entire finger pointing out of the conversation. It also allows you to leave your emotions at home where they can be unproductive on their own time. When this approach is taken, the person listening will be more open to hear what you have to say and will feel less defensive. Also, they will be more attentive to what you have to say. Blaming the other person only alienates them and puts them on the defensive. So the fear you had about them getting angry usually ends up happening anyway.

The next time we see Benaiah he is in a winner take all, no holds barred cage death match with a seven foot Egyptian. This Egyptian was one big dude! Not only was he big but he was carrying a big spear. The Bible says it was like a "weavers beam" for those of you who might need a clarification: the Egyptian's spear was the "Weapon of Mass Destruction" of the day. It was long, sharp, and most likely did its job very well. I like to think the Egyptian may have been ugly too because big, ugly, threatening opponents always make a better story, but I digress. So he was a big man with a big spear but we see again that Benaiah's actions were consistent with his character. Benaiah went to him – he didn't wait for the Egyptian to come to him. Benaiah must have been well schooled in some form of martial arts because the Bible says he confronted the Egyptian, plucked the spear from his grasp, and slew him with his own spear. In my mind this would have required him to be fast, strong and with a healthy lack of fear. All the odds were against him but he confronted the Egyptian head-on. He may have been scared but I like to think he was more afraid of the consequences if he didn't do something than if he did. We are not sure why he was even up against this giant of a man, but knowing what we do about Benaiah's character, it was probably for some offense against the people under his care. Nothing challenges a Mighty Man of Valor more than a threat to that which has been placed under our care. In times past I have been the recipient of many degrading comments and even some physical threats that didn't bother me half as much as someone making a threatening comments to my wife or family. Say all you want to about me but should you want to take it to the level where you impugn the character of my wife, or my friends, or my God, then you and I will go head-to-head over it. We will always fight harder for those we love than we will for ourselves, it's one of those interesting little quirks that God designed us with.

Benaiah didn't fight just to fight – he did everything with a purpose and for a cause. I don't think he was the kind of person who liked violence for the sake of violence but rather was willing to commit acts of violence when there was no other recourse. We have points in our lives where we must draw the line. People's lives and souls are at stake. Benaiah didn't wait for the two Moabite warriors to come along and kill someone he loved. He took the fight to them. He didn't wait for the lion to come and steal his livestock away in the night. He confronted the lion in his own environment. Even in the case of the Egyptian, we find that no matter what the offense might have been, Benaiah was ready and willing to what needed to be done and to carry it to its fullest extent. The bottom line is that he was ready and willing to take action and to take said action first.

One interesting point about all three scenarios described here that I'd like to point out is that in each one Benaiah was alone. A Mighty Man knows that there sometimes comes a point when he must stand alone. Sometimes no matter how great the cause or how important it may be, you, as man, may have to carry it alone. Many will say that they will help, but when it comes right down to it you may find yourself standing on the field alone and it will be up to you whether or not the mission is accomplished. Benaiah stood alone against the Moabites. No one else was with him in the pit and when he took on the lion, it was Mano a Mano. We may have to do what we know to be right without the backing or support of our family and friends. We may have to go against all the odds heaped against us to accomplish that which we know to be of the most benefit to the very people who go against us. We have all heard it described as "standing in the gap". The mere fact that a gap exists leads one to wonder where the failure started. Filling the gap means sometimes standing alone in a place where no one else is willing to or wants to go. It sometimes means ignoring the critics and moving forward anyway.

As daunting as this sounds, there are some things you as a man can do to ensure your success:

Know Yourself
On the Temple of Apollo at Delphi are inscribed two words: Know Thyself. Many scholars believe that the inscription may refer to the Greek ideal of understanding human behavior, morals, and thought, because

ultimately to understand oneself is to understand others as well. You must become aware of your own limitations in order to become aware of the limitations of others. A warrior must know what his own needs are and what he is capable of before he can help the troops with theirs. Begin by asking yourself the hard questions. Why do I act the way I do? Why do I think the way I do? If I were faced with this particular situation, what would I do? Decide what is important to you and what is not. Figure out what you enjoy, what you don't, and more importantly, why. Work to discover your capabilities and your weaknesses; analyze your motives and your actions. The more you know about yourself the more confident you will become; the more confident you are the more you will be able to lift up those who doubt themselves. Analyze whether your talk matches your walk but always remember that truly self-confident leaders don't need to advertise, their actions say it all.

One day my wife and I were driving across town to babysit our godson, Tyler. Normally, getting from one side of town to the other was not an issue because there was a "shortcut" which we used all the time. For some reason, which neither of us can remember, we were in separate vehicles and Lisa decided to take the long way across town whereas I took the "shortcut." I made it to our destination before her, and when Lisa did finally arrive she was pale, shaking, wide-eyed, and obviously upset. When we asked her what was the matter, Lisa explained that some guys in a van had tried to run her off the road.

Apparently, while driving through town along the main route something happened that incensed four male occupants of a van, and they began driving in a threatening manner toward Lisa. It may have been a case of mistaken identity or maybe these male antagonists may have just felt like scaring someone. For all we know they may have had too much to drink. You notice that I refer to them as "males" and not "men." Anyone can be a male but it takes someone willing to uphold and defend a certain set of values to be a "man". Anyway, they pulled up beside her on the shoulder, all the while shouting and gesturing, and then aggressively crossed three lanes to pull up beside her in the median with the van doors open continuing to yell at her. Part of her conscious mind was trying to figure out why this was happening and the other part was attempting to figure a way out of it. The males in the van couldn't get around her due to the fact that there were other people in other vehicles in the other lanes. These other people in traffic observed all of this taking place but chose to do nothing. This all came to a head at a traffic light where these four individuals exited the van and started moving toward Lisa's car, shouting obscenities and still making threatening gestures.

You can imagine Lisa's level of anxiety at that moment; it was four against one and that one is a woman who still doesn't understand how all of this came to be in the first place. In one of those rare moments when God lets us know that he is always watching and always protecting us, the light turned green. Lisa took off in more of a hurry than is normally allowed by law leaving the pack of morons just standing. She thought she had escaped when she suddenly saw that they had caught up to her and were barreling up the median to reach her. She sped up, and at that instant the van tried to cut across in front of her, but mistimed the maneuver and had to cut behind her instead. At that point she decided to pull over and seek help when she noticed they had stopped some distance back. Apparently, when they had cut across behind her, they hit a pickup truck driven by what we city folk affectionately refer to as "rednecks." Before any of you fly off the handle and accuse me of stereotyping people or using derogatory comments know this: I myself have been labeled as such and proudly stand by my affiliation. In my mind, on that day, these rednecks became heroes.

You know who I am talking about. We see them all the time driving large trucks with even larger tires. They are rolling billboards for all things NASCAR and horsepower related. They are conservative, God-fearing, Bible-believing, country music promoting outstanding members of society who will defend country and flag at the drop of a hat. The men in the truck were a bit upset, to say the least, about the behavior of the males in the van toward a defenseless female. In addition to that, the van guys had just damaged the redneck's truck. Their answer to this injustice was to exit their vehicle and proceed to pull the males out of their van and beat the stuffing out of them. One of the pickup truck guys (both of whom we later decided were Mighty Men) asked Lisa if she was OK and then told her she should leave so that she wouldn't have any further involvement should the police be called. She could not believe it. As she drove away she could see them through the rear view mirror continuing to rain

49

discipline down upon the occupants of the van, who had obviously picked the wrong guys to mess with. Needless to say, when she told me this story I was ready to jump in my truck (notice the reference here?) and drive back to join the fun. However, Lisa and I will forever be grateful to God and to the "redneck men" that He allowed to make a difference in her life that day.

Right now you are asking yourself; what does that have to do with anything we are discussing? These men may not have thought their day would develop like it did, but when it did they were ready to do what needed to be done, when it needed to be done. I am sure when they left the house that morning they didn't ask themselves how and where they might find cause to uphold and defend the rights of those who could not stand for themselves but because of their positive, there-will-be-no-wrong-done-here-today attitude they were able in a short period of time to size up the situation, quickly determine what was important and take action. They left the house that morning as ordinary citizens but came home as modern day patriots.

> *This is no war of chieftains or of princes, of dynasties or national ambition; it is a war of peoples and of causes. There are vast numbers, not only in this island but in every land, who will render faithful service in this war but whose names will never be known, whose deeds will never be recorded. This is a war of the Unknown Warriors. – Winston Churchill [BBC Broadcast, London, 14 July 1940]*

Here are some helpful hints that may come in handy the next time you are asked to act:

Know Your Mission
Always know what you are trying to accomplish. Can you state without hesitation what your purpose is? A clear sense of purpose provides a solid foundation for successful future actions. Do you know from one day to the next what your next course of action may be and have you determined how that course of action furthers your goals? Are you focused on the mission?

Your mission plan needs to be consistent with those ideals that you value most. Goals that do not support your core values will eventually become more of a deterrent than an advantage.

There is a constant battle raging within and all around us for our attention. The only hope we have of winning in this struggle is to develop and establish goals. In order to do this we must know where we are going, and what we are going to accomplish. Any other course is a recipe for distraction and, just as distraction can kill on the battlefield, it can knock you off track from accomplishing your mission.

Know Your Message

Do you know what kind of signals you are sending to people? Have you ever had someone approach you and you knew very well that they were angry for some reason? How did you know if they didn't say anything? Were their hands clenched into fists? Was their face turning red? Were their eyes slightly bulging? Our body language will transmit more to the people around us than our mouths ever will. People will know when we are hesitant, nervous, or indecisive. I had a friend once who told me I needed to work on my "game face", which he described as the outward physical expression of what I was thinking at the moment. When I was angry my actions told him so. When I was sad my actions reflected it. Do your actions uphold the message you are trying to deliver? Are they a good example to the people around you? Always remember that your actions will deliver a far more powerful message to the world around you than your words ever could

I once read a story about a pastor who knew when to take action and decided to do so decisively. Joe Barron was a minister of adults at Prestonwood Baptist Church which is a mega church in Plano, Texas. Barron was arrested in a police sting operation as he attempted to solicit sex from an officer posing online as a 13-year-old girl. Within two days of learning of the arrest, Jack Graham, the senior pastor of Prestonwood, addressed his congregation about the scandal from the pulpit. He did not try to defend the disgraced minister; he did not speak of all the good things Rev. Barron had done in the years he had been with the church nor did he call for forgiveness. He did not say that the pastor was going off for counseling and would be back in ministry soon as a "wounded healer." He didn't blame the world for Barron's fall and he made no excuses or attempt at cover-up.   All that was left was just clear, firm, sober action.

In his address, he simply said that the facts had been considered, and the accused had been asked to resign.   He acknowledged the challenge but thanked God for the solution.   He challenged the church members to uphold their own Christian standards of morality and he even thanked the media for their coverage. As one editorial described it:

> *"Because of this, it's probably safe to say that the Prestonwood congregation has a lot more faith in its clergy today than it might have otherwise. In the end, the real scandal in cases like this comes not from the sins and crimes of sexual offenders. No church will ever be free of that.   The truly damaging scandals arise when leaders mishandle these crises by failing to treat them with the gravity they deserve. Many in church authority have failed their calling and their congregations under similar conditions, through defensiveness, dissimulation and deferring hard decisions."*

True Mighty Men don't allow feelings to influence what needs to get done today.   I am sure Pastor Graham felt overwhelmed and disappointed during the crisis in his church but he didn't allow those feelings to dictate the actions necessary nor did he allow those feelings to become outward expressions via his actions. The key to your success is using your actions to influence your attitude. When you discipline yourself to take the actions that must be taken, your attitude will begin to change and allow you to further alter your actions. Your work habits will develop in direct proportion to your goals. How badly you want to achieve your goals will determine how much work you are be willing to do.

When my wife and I went into business for ourselves, a portion of our business model required me to have to talk to complete strangers at times. At the time I was an extreme introvert, which is to say my attitude was not conducive to taking action when necessary.   I heard a statement that basically said that if I wanted to change my outcome I needed to change my habits so I went and started doing the one thing that I feared the most, talking to people. Before long I found myself actually enjoying it more and more. My attitude had changed so much that I went looking for people to talk to. When we fail to do what we know we should do, our attitude is affected negatively. When we do what we know we should do, our attitude is affected positively. In the end, your actions will influence your attitude, which will in turn affect your actions. Nothing will do more to determine a Mighty Man's ability to lead others as the actions he takes on a daily basis to lead others.

Chapter 5
Mighty Men are known by Their Attitudes

If you are distressed by anything external, the pain is not due to the thing itself, but to your estimate of it; and this you have the power to revoke at any moment. - Marcus Aurelius

When I was growing up my parents used to tell me that I could do anything I wanted if I just put my mind to it. The problem was that I never knew what I was supposed to be putting my mind to, so I ended up putting it to either everything or nothing. Since I had no plan of action, my attention was scattered amongst various interests, none of which were getting my full attention; that lack of focus led to wasted time and effort. Having a great attitude is a good thing but it will not change the facts in your life. It will not reverse the numbers in your checkbook, nor will it keep the lights on when the bill is overdue. What it will do is make a difference in your approach to life. Our performance is directly related to our expectations, and it is difficult to conduct ourselves in a manner inconsistent with our expectations. Your attitude is more important than your past, your education, your financial statements, or even your present circumstances. It is more important than what you look like or what you do. Attitude will make or break a Mighty Man of Valor.
(Do you really intend to say (above) that other people's expectations for us have as much importance as our own expectations for ourselves?)

In The Anatomy of an Illness: As Perceived by the Patient, Norman Cousins tells of being hospitalized with a rare, crippling disease. When he was diagnosed as incurable, Cousins checked out of the hospital. Aware of the harmful effects that negative emotions can have on the body, Cousins reasoned the reverse was true. So he borrowed a movie projector and prescribed his own treatment, consisting of Marx Brothers films and old "Candid Camera" reruns. It didn't take long for him to discover that 10 minutes of laughter provided two hours of pain free sleep. Amazingly, his debilitating disease was eventually reversed. After the account of his victory appeared in the New England Journal of Medicine, Cousins received more than 3000 letters from appreciative physicians throughout the world. Cousins found that laughter allowed him to change his attitude or his perception of the predicament he was in. His attitude allowed him to see his world with optimism and overcome any negativity formed by his illness.

I heard a statement a long time ago that basically stated that I could not always choose what happened to me but I could always choose what happened in me. Focusing your attitude on what you can control will help you overcome the things you cannot control.

> *A chaplain was speaking to a soldier on a cot in a hospital. "You have lost an arm in the great cause," he said. "No," said the soldier with a smile. "I didn't lose it--I gave it."*

In ancient times, the Bible celebrated the deeds of Mighty Men of Valor, who possessed the stamina to fight from sun-up to sun-down. It was nothing for them to enter the field of battle before dawn and hope to still be standing at sunset, all the while doing their levelheaded best to overcome the enemy. The lesson learned is that they didn't give up because to give in meant certain death. They did not have the luxury of taking a lunch break if they were tired, or a trip to the bathroom when the need called. They looked deep down inside and found the courage to continue. The world needs courageous men and it needs big men. I'm not talking about the physical size of the man but rather about men big in mind, heart, and spirit. We need men whose faith is big, whose vision can carry them through complicated problems and whose spirit can overcome any challenge. We need men big enough to love, compassionate enough to act, and secure enough to risk whatever is necessary. We need men who are big on action. In short, we need big men with big attitudes.

All of us have experienced the occasional wake-up call in our lives. None ever come like a gentle breeze wafting slowly into our lives but rather are akin to the crack of a two-by-four across the back of our skulls to get our attention. Some wake up calls for a man might include:

- My children are out of control and I just figured that out.
- My wife has been distant for years, and I just realized it.
- I don't have a close relationship with my children and they're almost grown.
- I haven't been listening to God and just realized the reason.

- I haven't prayed for a week and just realized why
- I am involved in a sinful habit and someone close to me just found out.
- I am trying to find happiness in places where none exist.
- I just realized the opportunity to make a difference has passed.

How many times have we as men had these wake-up calls in our lives? How many times have we seen or heard the warning bells indicating that not all is right in the kingdom? How many times have we struggled to maintain the proper attitude when faced with overwhelming challenges that threaten to destroy us?

In the Book of Job, Job is described as a rich, blessed man who fears God and lives righteously. God blesses him with great health, a huge family, a large estate, and every material possession available at the time. The story opens with the impression that Job is the very best there is. He sits on the verge of sinlessness and only because of the human condition which makes anything else near impossible, does he not become more. Satan challenges God's opinion of Job by implying that He has erred because human beings are incapable of a completely selfless love of God. Satan thinks that they love God only for what they can get from him. Satan challenges God to create a situation of undeserved suffering in order to settle this question of righteousness and reward. God chooses Job as his personal champion in this trial by ordeal and authorizes the destruction of his lifestyle.

God allows Satan to bring the house down on Job. All his property is taken away, his possessions are destroyed, his family is scattered and he is made to suffer in his health. Job turns to God for answers for the evil in his world. He has faith that God must have a hidden purpose which he has not revealed. God remains silent but Job still chooses his own attitude. You see, Satan put one stipulation on God in this little game. God could not reveal to Job or anyone else the reason for the calamity that has befallen him. Job's entire material existence is gone with no light at the end of the tunnel so-to-speak. He cries out to God asking the reason for this sudden turn of events and fortune but, alas, no answer comes.

How many times have we been in Jobs shoes? How many times have all our dreams and goals gone up in smoke and we blamed God for our misfortune? How many times have we done everything right but yet nothing seems to go our way? God presents us with challenges so that we may have opportunities to really grow through them. He opens doors in some places and closes others to us. He wants us to overcome and conquer, which is hard to do if we don't have something to overcome or conquer. Job elected not to condemn God but to adjust his attitude and overcome whatever Satan dished out. He recognized that there is evil in the world and he is just as susceptible to it as the next guy. In the end, God richly blesses and restores Job, giving him more than he had before. His life becomes his testimony.

Things to Remember About Your Attitude:

Attitude is a Choice
Your attitude is a choice. It is made every second of every minute of every day. Sometimes we make the choice to have the proper attitude and sometimes we don't....it's that simple. Our vision for what we want to accomplish, whether it be for our family or business, is directly related to the attitude we have while we are attempting to complete that vision. If we go into it with a bad attitude then we will realize a bad outcome. However, the clearer your attitude, the stronger your emotions; the stronger your emotions, the greater your commitment; the greater your commitment, the tougher your challenges; the tougher your challenges, the richer your rewards. We cannot change other people's attitudes but we can influence them with our own. We cannot change people's actions but we can change our own.

Many years ago I was working for a telecommunication firm that was going through some tough financial times. There had been a number of layoffs but I felt relatively safe in my position because of promises that were made to me by the management staff. Lisa and I planned a vacation that summer and decided not to let the insecurity around us affect whether we chose to go or not. The Board of Directors for this company didn't ask for my help in getting into the tough situation and therefore were not asking me how to get out of it either. We spent a great week in Las Vegas developing memories that we cherish even today but on the last day of our time away I received a phone call. My supervisor called to let me know that he was really sorry but that when I returned they would most likely have to prepare what's called an exit package for me. They were laying me off! I couldn't believe it at first, and to be honest was really shaken and angry at the same time. I honestly thought I was safe. After telling Lisa what happened and weighing our options we both decided that we were not going to let it shake us. We CHOSE not to let the circumstances affect our attitude. We enjoyed the last day of our vacation, and over the weekend before I was suppose to return to work I forced myself not to think about what was going to happen on Monday. As it turned out, on the day of my return my supervisor called me into his office and told me that they had been able to work out a solution and I could keep my job for a bit longer. He apologized to me for putting me through any mental anguish the situation may have caused. I told him not to give it another thought because I had not until the day before we met. He was amazed that I was able to maintain such a positive attitude in such trying times.

God will test you like that sometimes. He will present you with challenges that can drastically alter your attitude and therefore affect your testimony to those around you. He will sometimes present you with situations and options that will push you near the edge. It is up to you which path you will choose. It has been said that we cannot change the inevitable but we can choose our attitude. And so it is with you... you have complete control over your attitude. You will find that the toughest adversary to overcome regarding choices in your attitude will not be the ones in front of you but rather the ones inside of you.

Attitude Develops Perspective
There's a charming story that Thomas Wheeler, CEO of the Massachusetts Mutual Life Insurance Company, tells about himself: He and his wife were driving along an interstate highway when he noticed that their car was low on gas. Wheeler got off the highway at the next exit and soon found a rundown gas station with just one gas pump. He asked the lone attendant to fill the tank and check the oil; then went for a little walk around the station to stretch his legs. As he was returning to the car, he noticed that the attendant and Wheeler's wife were engaged in an animated conversation. The conversation stopped as he paid the attendant. But as he was getting back into the car, he saw the attendant wave and heard him

say, "It was great talking to you." As they drove out of the station, Wheeler asked his wife if she knew the man, she said she went to high school with the attendant and, in fact, the two had dated steadily for about a year. "Boy, were you lucky that I came along," bragged Wheeler, "If you had married him, you'd be the wife of a gas station attendant instead of the wife of a chief executive officer." "My dear," replied his wife, "if I had married him, he'd be the chief executive officer and you'd be the gas station attendant." Mrs. Wheeler had a different perspective than her husband.

Have you ever noticed those people in the office who are always having a bad day – no matter what? Their alarm clock went off too early or didn't go off at all. Their car wouldn't start or made the infamous $600 dollar noise on the way to the office. They listened to the radio, hoping to hear that the universe had come to an end last night and work was canceled. Their dog made a buffet out of their dress shoes and the cat used their pants as a new scratching post. Their newspaper apparently was delivered to the house next door and when they did get it, they found out that the world had gone to hell in a hand basket. They got up early to beat the rush hour but everyone else in the city had the same idea. They chose to eat at the dashboard diner and got something on their shirt. Their usual parking space in the shade now has a delivery truck parked in it. They act like they ate pizza, ice cream and chocolate cake together for breakfast. It doesn't matter if it's first thing in the morning or right before quitting time, they are grumpy and irritable. No amount of joy in their life ever seems to brighten their attitude. They always see the world as revolving around them instead of the other way around. They see their problems as the greatest tragedy to ever been inflicted upon any one human being. They are need of a change of perspective.

A bad day for someone else should never translate into a bad day for us; we as Mighty Men must always strive to maintain a positive attitude. By maintaining a proper positive attitude we are be able to maintain a proper positive perspective. It's when we lose perspective that the trouble usually starts. Job never lost his perspective. No matter what was going on around him, he stayed focused on worshiping God; we Mighty Men need to remember his example. When it seems that all hell is breaking loose around us we must remember that we are being watched.

I heard a story some years back about a traveler who was driving in the country one day when he saw an old man sitting on a fence rail watching the cars go by. Stopping to pass the time of day, the traveler said, "I never could stand living out here. You don't see anything, and I'm sure you don't travel like I do. I'm on the go all the time." The old man on the fence looked down at the stranger and drawled, "I can't see much difference in what I'm doing and what you're doing. I sit on the fence and watch the autos go by and you sit in your auto and watch the fences go by. It's just the way you look at things."

The biography of Colonel George "Bud" Day illustrates how our attitude makes a difference in how we face challenges and helps us maintain perspective. Bud Day became famous after surviving for over five and a half years in a North Vietnamese prison camp during the Vietnam War. On August 26, 1967, Day was directing an air strike against a surface-to-air missile (SAM) site west of Dong Hoi, 20 miles north of the Demilitarized Zone in North Vietnam from the backseat of an F-100. Day was on his 65th mission and acting as check pilot for Captain Kippenham, who was flying as aircraft commander for the first time. 37mm antiaircraft fire crippled the aircraft, forcing the crew to eject. In the ejection, Day's right arm was broken in three places when he struck the side of the cockpit, and he also experienced serious eye and back injuries.

Kippenham was rescued, but Day was unable to contact the rescue helicopter by survival radio and was quickly captured by local North Vietnamese militia fighters. They stripped the injured pilot of his boots and flight suit and force-marched him to an underground shelter for initial interrogation. When he refused to cooperate, his captors staged a mock execution and then hung him from a rafter by his feet for several pain-filled hours followed by nights in a hole outside the shelter. The Vietnamese marched him north, stopping at various villages and hamlets so that the local population could take turns beating and kicking him. On his fifth night, when he was still within twenty miles of the DMZ, Day escaped from his captors despite his serious injuries. He attempted to escape because he took the military Code of conduct seriously, including the section on capture, that says,

"As an individual, a member of the armed forces may never voluntarily surrender. When isolated and no longer able to inflict casualties on the enemy, the American soldier has an obligation to evade capture and rejoin friendly forces."

Although stripped of his boots and flight suit, Day crossed the DMZ back into South Vietnam, becoming the only US prisoner to escape from North Vietnam. Within two miles of the US. Marine fire base at Con Thien and after 12-15 days of evading, he was captured again, this time by a Viet Cong patrol that wounded him in the leg and hand with gunfire.

Taken back to his original camp, Day was tortured for escaping, breaking his right arm again. He then was moved to what was affectionately named the "Hanoi Hilton", where he was periodically beaten, starved, and tortured for six weeks straight. His captors beat, hung, twisted, smashed, slapped and punched Day, sometimes for more than 24 hours in a single session. The notion of giving up, of course, penetrated many times through the pain but Day's sense of mission and honor reinforced his will not to surrender. He thought of his wife, his children, fishing trips, happy hour, anything that could take his mind off the incredible pain inflicted by his tormentors. While he and others took turns filling the role of senior officer within the camp, Bud Day never let those under his command see him with a less than positive attitude. They had all been stretched to their physical and mental limits but he constantly reminded himself of the goal: to return with honor. He continually praised them and attempted to lift their spirits so that they may fight just one more day. He knew that his men were waiting to see how he would react. Would he give in? Would he become depressed? Bud's never give up; can-do attitude inspired his fellow POWs to adopt the same mindset. He endured the brutality for 67 months and never betrayed his comrades or country while living in a virtual hell.

Bud Day's attitude and perspective were never diminished despite the horror he had endured. Constantly aware that he and his comrades might not make it out alive, Bud decided what was more important was how they lived while they were there. His goal was the eventual freedom of every man under his command but he wanted everyone to reach that point with their self-respect intact. They returned home, having bent but never broken to the enemy's demands. He taught his men through his actions that their attitudes would save their lives. On March 14, 1973, Day and many of his fellow mighty men were released after five years and seven months as North Vietnamese prisoners. Within three days Day was reunited with his wife, Doris, and their four children. On March 14, 1976, President Gerald Ford awarded Day the Medal of Honor for his personal bravery while a captive in North Vietnam. Colonel Day served his country in three different wars and is the Air Force's most highly decorated officer. He holds almost 70 military decorations, of which more than 50 are for combat. They include the Air Force Cross, the Distinguished Service Medal, and the Silver Star. He wears 12 campaign battle stars.

Attitude is Not a Substitute for Competence or Experience.
(Don't you mean that attitude is at least as important as competence? That attitude is a pathway to competence? Speaking of that, maybe we should use the term "excellence" instead of "competence") attitude can certainly be a factor in the development of competence but one cannot be substituted for the other. Attitude without competence and vise versa is like owning a gun without bullets. It won't fire no matter how many times you pull the trigger. I like 'experience' but 'excellence' would be a good fit as well.

No matter how good you are at something, it will never substitute for a great attitude. You can be great at a particular task but if you have a poor attitude you will not perform that task well for very long. You will quickly become discouraged, which will affect your performance. On the flip side, you can be mediocre at something but have a great attitude and still realize great success because the people around you will remember your attitude long before they remember your work. Have you ever noticed that real competence appears mostly in tough times? Who is willing to make the hard decisions? Who has the confidence to stay the course? Who has the ability to shine even in the darkest times? These are the most necessary questions for someone striving for competence. It all really comes down to being able to answer the age old question, can I deliver what people need or are looking for? The ability to answer these questions is determined by your attitude. A poor attitude will limit you in the development of competence in any field and will deter you from taking the necessary steps and making the necessary sacrifices to develop competence.

You don't become competent through a college education or by duplicating the actions of others. You become competent by doing the things that others are unwilling to do. You don't become competent at driving a car or riding a motorcycle by reading the manual, no matter what your attitude towards it may be. You become that way by actually driving or riding the motorcycle. You try, you fail and you adjust. Competence gives you the ability to see every detail of any situation and deliver just the right solution at just the right time.

Psychologists refer to the "Four Stages of Competence" model which relates to the psychological states involved in the process of progressing from incompetence to competence in a skill. The learning model states that whenever an individual develops a new skill; they go through four distinct levels of learning to build that deficiency into a competency. These Phases are:

Phase I—Unconscious Incompetence
("We don't know that we don't know")
The individual is not aware of a particular skill or behavior that they are deficient in. We sometimes refer to it as ignorant bliss. People deny the usefulness of the particular skill since both the skill and its application are out of their realm of comprehension.

Phase II—Conscious Incompetence
("We know that we don't know")
The individual becomes aware of the specific skill that must be learned. Usually this awareness is brought on by our own trials and errors. The person will fumble about and realize that he have much to learn in order to master the new skill. We make most of our mistakes at this stage.

Phase III—Conscious Competence
("We know that we know")
After enough training and repetition, we are able to execute the skill or behavior with a certain level of proficiency at will. This proficiency does not come automatically. We still have to concentrate on performing the specific task in order to execute it properly.

Phase IV—Unconscious Competence
("We don't know that we know")
At this stage, the skill is automatic and comes naturally without any conscious thought. We have practiced the skill so much now that it enters the subconscious mind and requires no mental focus to execute it. It becomes second-nature like walking and breathing but now can articulate it to others.

Let me give you a practical application as to how the four stages work. For this example, I will use my friend Glen's skill of riding a motorcycle to illustrate the progression:

Unconscious incompetence = Non-Rider. Glen is unaware of the skill necessary to ride a motorcycle because he has never ridden one before. He does not know there is skill behind riding a motorcycle because it is not a part of Glen's life. He has no worries about not having a competency in it.

Conscious Incompetence = Aware Non-Rider. Glen becomes aware of the skills necessary when a friend offers to take him for a ride one day. Glen sees the concentration and sense of balance that his friend has and decides "It's not as easy as it looks." Glen says to himself. "If I want to ever ride a motorcycle on my own I am going to have to practice." Glen at this point is consciously aware that he is an inexperienced and unskilled rider. It becomes his motivation to practice.

Conscious Competence = Student Rider. With sweaty palms and a lump in his throat Glen convinces a friend to let him practice on his motorcycle in an empty parking lot. He rides in straight lines and through curves becoming familiar with the weight and motion of the motorcycle. He signs up for an introductory class designed to teach competency while riding a motorcycle. After the class, he again goes out to the empty parking lot to practice. Glen becomes a competent rider, but he must consciously focus on the balance and maneuverability in order to apply them when he is riding.

Unconscious Competence = Super Rider. Glen is now an extremely competent rider even to the point where he now can take his wife Veronica as passenger on long trips. He no longer thinks about the balance or techniques necessary to avoid obstacles in his path. He is always aware but they have been relegated to his subconscious. Glen can now ride and talk to Veronica at the same time. Glen has practiced riding enough to the point where he does not have to focus on each and every detail to perform that skill with proficiency.

Having a great attitude about riding a motorcycle will never replace the competency or experience necessary to keep you as the rider and your passenger safe while on the road.

Attitude Makes a Difference in Your Approach to Life.
I read the following story and thought it may be useful as an example of great attitudes verses not so great attitudes.

A clergyman, a doctor, and a business consultant were playing golf together one day and were waiting for a particularly slow group ahead. The business consultant exclaimed, "What's with these people? We've been waiting over half and hour! It's a complete disgrace." The doctor agreed, "They're hopeless, I've never seen such a rabble on a golf course." The clergyman spotted the approaching greens keeper and asked him what was going on, "What's happening with that group ahead of us? They're surely too slow and useless to be playing, aren't they?" The greens keeper replied, "Oh, yes, that's a group of blind fire-fighters. They lost their sight saving our clubhouse from a fire last year, so we always let them play for free anytime." The three golfers fell silent for a moment. The clergyman said, "Oh dear, that's so sad. I shall say some special prayers for them tonight." The doctor added, rather meekly, "That's a good thought. I'll get in touch with an ophthalmic surgeon friend of mine to see if there's anything that can be done for them." After pondering the situation for a few seconds, the business consultant turned to the greens keeper and asked, "Why can't they play at night?"

It sounds amusing but is indicative of how our attitudes are not only a matter of choice but also how they affect our approach to life. The clergyman was concerned for the spiritual well-being of the golfers while the doctor thought of a way to help by utilizing his network. The business consultant just wanted to play golf.

Lisa and I have had many well-meaning (I assume) friends who have offered us various forms of advice over the years such as "I wouldn't do that, you might lose your shirt" or "don't get your hopes up. It will only worsen your disappointment when it fails" I especially love this one: "Even though I have never tried that, let me offer you some advice." I am sure most of them were well-meaning but even the best endeavors will begin to crumble under a constant onslaught of negative attitudes such as this. Our parents are great people. As kids they think we never listen to them but because of their examples I learned that all my accomplishments would come as a direct result of a lot of hard work and whatever my attitude might be. No matter how bad their situation may have been I never heard my parents speak ill of it or mouth a negative comment towards anyone involved. If they were facing financial troubles we never knew about it. If someone in the family had a physical challenge it was always put to us in the most positive light. Come to think of it I can only remember one instance when I ever saw my parents have an argument. My Mom was capable of finding something positive in almost any situation and my Dad never backed down from any confrontation. Outside my wife Lisa, he was the most emotionally strong individual I have ever had the privilege to know.

Right now, inside of you, is the power to achieve anything and everything that anyone else ever has. If you want to be a great husband, the ability is inside you. If you want to be a better father, all the answers lie within you. Let's say you want to start your own business and build it into a corporate powerhouse, the foundation to do so is inside of you. All that is necessary is for you to start with a great attitude. Don't get me wrong here, it will not guarantee you any success in any of these ventures. Some people have great attitudes with which they achieve great things and some people have mediocre attitudes and their lives are a reflection of it. Others have absolutely horrid attitudes and trouble never seems to leave them but whether you have a great attitude or a mediocre one, no measure of success can be realized without a decent amount of work.

A very old lady looked in the mirror one morning. She had three remaining hairs on her head, and being a positive soul, she said, "I think I'll braid my hair today." So she braided her three hairs, and she had a great day. Some days later, looking in the mirror one morning, preparing for her day, she saw that she had only two hairs remaining. "Hmm, two hairs... I fancy a center parting today." She duly parted her two hairs, and as ever, she had a great day. A week or so later, she saw that she had just one hair left on her head. "One hair huh...," she mused, "I know a pony-tail will be perfect." And again she had a great day. The next morning she looked in the mirror. She was completely bald. "Finally bald huh," she said to herself, "How wonderful! I won't have to waste time doing my hair any more."

We all have the ability to achieve proper attitudes if we will only learn to keep our thoughts focused on the things we want and off the things we do not want. You, as a Mighty Man need to take possession of your mind and direct it to the attitude of your choosing. Some think that spending time thinking about ways of correcting a bad situation means that you run the risk of having the bad situation affect your attitude. You might become overwhelmed by it or that it may begin to affect you in a negative manner. Fortunately the human mind doesn't work like that. If you dwell on the challenge you will do nothing but make a bad situation worse. But if you ponder ways of correcting the situation your mind will eventually produce a solution. Rob Gilbert once said *"Losers visualize the penalties of failure. Winners visualize the rewards of success"*

Chapter 6
Mighty Men Build and Protect Their Thoughts

"Thinking is the hardest work there is, which is the probable reason why so few engage in it" – Henry Ford

Fifty-six thousand. According to the National Science Foundation, that's how many thoughts you and I have each day. (I didn't sit around counting mine). Our thoughts range from what the weather is like to sex, sometimes at the same time. So you have to ask yourself, "How many of these thoughts are actually under my control?" Or perhaps even more important, "How often am I actually controlled by these thoughts?" Have you ever heard someone say, "I don't want to think about it right now?" People who make that statement are really saying, "I don't want to take responsibility for it." Mighty Men of Valor take responsibility for their lives - the good and the bad - and it can all be traced to the thoughts we entertain day-in and day-out. Our thoughts directly impact our character and our attitude - we are what we think!!! Thought and action go hand in hand, together, they allow us to model our world and to deal with it effectively and accordingly based on our dreams, plans, and desires. We sometimes refer to them as ideas or imaginings. Some tell us to protect our dreams because they are fragile. Dreams are not fragile; they are strong and resilient because we protect and strengthen them with our thoughts.

Thinking involves the mental manipulation of information, such as when we form concepts, engage in problem solving, reason, and make decisions. In short, our thoughts define who we are and what we do. A Mighty Man of Valor is an aggressive thinker – always anticipating and analyzing, while attempting to make good decisions and judgments along the way. To some those decisions may, at times, seem a bit unconventional. It's sometimes referred to as "thinking outside the box." This phrase often refers to novel, creative and smart thinking. The idea of thinking outside the box is that unconventional problem solving could be used to solve issues where conventional thinking has failed. Thinking inside the box means accepting the status quo. For example, Charles H. Duell, Director of the US Patent Office, once said, "Everything that can be invented has been invented." That was in 1899, clearly he was in the box!

I remember once when I was in the Boy Scouts, I was attempting to earn what was called the Wilderness Survival Merit Badge. In order to earn this particular award one must be able to establish priorities for survival in a wilderness environment, avoid panic and maintain a high degree of morale if lost. You must know how to find shelter, feed yourself, and protect yourself and your comrades without any of the modern conveniences. A scout must know how to think clearly whether he is cold and wet, hot and dry, no matter if he is on a mountain or in the middle of the ocean. He must be able to demonstrate the ability start a fire using three methods other than matches; he must know how to use signal mirrors and other attention-getting techniques; and he must spend a night in a shelter of his own construction while protecting himself against the elements, insects, reptiles, and other creepy crawly things. A scout must know which plants not to eat and where to find water.

My scoutmaster came up with an interesting situation that required my troop to spend an entire weekend, in groups of four, with nothing on us but our clothes, a rain poncho, a knife, and a half a pound of hamburger issued to each person. He took us to a very remote area of the woods, a location in which rescue would be near impossible if something should go wrong, and left us to survive on our own for three days. I know some of you right now are screaming "child abuse" but remember he was doing this with our parent's permission. If I was being abused I personally was ready to sign up for more; we were having a great time. Our group of four marched off into the woods to practice the skills we had been taught only in classroom settings up to this point. We found a small tree that had blown over in a past storm which we used to construct a lean-to. It wasn't really big enough for all four of us but we made it work. With shelter taken care of the next priority was water. Finding it wasn't a problem, figuring out what to put it in was. We quickly discovered that one of the rain ponchos worked great for transporting water. The problem was that we were now down to two because we used another on in the construction of the lean-to. Where the story gets interesting is when it came time to cook dinner. I was standing over our newly constructed fire pit watching the other groups trying to start their fires. Some were beating rocks together and others were rubbing sticks. Some were just sitting there wondering just how bad raw hamburger really was. My three amigos were debating what would be the most useful method so as to maximize their efforts when I reached into my pocket and pulled out a book of matches. They all just stared at me in disbelief as I proceeded to start our cooking fire. One of them says to me, "you're not supposed to have those. They're against the rules" to which I replied, "Are we going to eat rules or raw hamburger?"

Before long the other groups were coming over and asking if they could borrow a bit of our fire to light their own. I guess they never heard of rubbing two matches together. So we cooked our hamburgers and had a great evening. On a side note, never use a rock from the river to cook your hamburger on. The water inside the fissures of the rock gets hot and expands eventually causing the rock to explode taking your hamburger with it. Before the night was over we discovered our next great challenge. We ate all the hamburger. We had to. We didn't have any way to store it for later consumption. We started to wonder what we were going to do for the next two days. We knew what plants and berries we could eat but there was a big difference in what they looked like in the book and what they looked like in the woods. We were not hungry enough to experiment yet, that would come later. Sometime in the afternoon of the second day, we were HUNGRY. When our stomachs began their collective growling it sounded like an entire pack of bears were on their way. My buddies had begun their ritual whimpering and whining when I reached into my coat and pulled out a Butter Finger candy bar and began munching away. Again, my friends had that wide-eyed dumbfounded look. "You cannot have that here!" or "what about the rules?" was all I heard for 15 minutes. I began to wonder if I had not allied myself with three future lawyers. "So you guys don't want any?" was my only response. They proceeded to table their closing arguments until a later date at which point I began to dole out candy bars to the starving masses.

The point I am trying to make is that even though the purpose of this exercise was to teach us what it was like to live off the land it was also to see if we were capable of independent or original thinking under adverse circumstances. Were we able to solve the problems in ways that were outside the confines of the rules? Would we think or starve? You may never have to eat berries or sleep outside with nothing but your clothes and a poncho for protection but each and every day you will be presented with challenges that will require you think a bit differently than those around you. You will learn that just because one person's solution worked one time doesn't meant that it will work again or be the correct solution every time. This kind of out-of-the-box thinking serves a unique purpose, it motivates us and inspires others. It shows others that they can create dynamic, unusual solutions to their own challenges and that they don't have to accept the status quo.

Andrew Carnegie once said, *"The man who acquires the ability to take full possession of his own mind may take possession of anything else to which he is justly entitled."* Mighty Men know <u>who</u> they are, they know <u>what</u> they are and they know <u>why</u> they are. They differ from everyone around them in their perspective, their methods, their convictions, and their motives. They differ due to their vision, experiences, and attitude but most importantly they differ because of the way they think.

My Dad always told me to never go looking for a fight but should one ever find me, to deal with it hard and deal with it early. You make a quick decision and follow through with it, right or wrong. He taught me that a man should never sit back and let the other guy make a decision that might put you on the defensive. You should always be prepared to take the fight to the enemy or ready yourself to make a stand before they attack.

The best place to take a stand and fight in any battle is in the beginning – with your thought life. God gave us all two ends; one we could sit on and one we could think with. Whichever one you use the most will determine your success. Thoughts are things which eventually manifest themselves as actions. We are who we are in our minds first before we speak or act; how you think determines what you do. William James, developer of *pragmatism* said *"Changing the inner attitude of your mind can and will change the outer aspect of your life"*. Eventually, how you think about things will affect your ability to make decisions or the quality of the decisions made. Your thoughts, and therefore your actions, will affect your life and future generations that may look at your life as the example.

In 1 Chronicles 11 there is recorded an interesting story about David and three of his Mighty Men. These three men decide to break through the battle line of the Philistines in order to bring David a drink of water from the well at Bethlehem. Though David had longed for the water, he does not drink of it because of the danger the men exposed themselves to in order to give to him. It is a wonderful story of loyalty and devotion to a leader, and we can certainly learn from that, but more importantly it's a great example of well-defined thought processes being used to accomplish a mission. This is how it went down:

David and his men were battling the Philistines and he was practically imprisoned in a cave near Adullam. He came there after being expelled from the court of King Saul, and gathered together "every one that was in distress, and every one that was in debt, and every one that was discontented" (1 Sam. 22:2). The Philistines were garrisoned in Bethlehem and controlled the surrounding valley leaving David unable to get the water from the well in the city. He was thirsty; with the water of that well he had often refreshed himself as a youth, and without due thought he voiced his desire for it. It was really just the outward expression of his thoughts being manifested in his words. The city was the birthplace of David and the location where he was crowned as the king of Israel. The three mighty men heard David going on and on about how great it would be to have a drink from the well of Bethlehem. Many would have been ready to risk their lives in carrying out some service for the benefit of the kingdom as a whole; but these mighty men were ready to face death in order to do something that was wholly for the gratification of the desire of their king. Because either they had no concept of failure or just refused to dwell on it, they left camp one night, broke through the lines of the enemy at great risk, drew water from the well, and returned to their own encampment. Note that it describes them as breaking through the lines, not sneaking through or stealthily maneuvering past the camp guards using some ruse such as a disguise. They didn't try to pass through the camp undetected like Ninjas. They simply went in, fought their way through, and brought David his water!

These three mighty men knew in their minds first that they could overcome and conquer any challenge that the Philistines could throw at them and they were willing to put that confidence to the test. They didn't sit around and analyze the repercussions or debate the possible outcomes. They didn't complain to anyone about the possibility someone might get hurt or worse. They didn't go ask their friends or their wives if they thought it was a good idea. They just stepped up, stepped out and stepped forward because they knew mentally and physically they could do it and there was nothing that could stop them. They did it for their love of their king, but more importantly as an example to those in David's command who might have been thinking this whole endeavor was a fool's errand. They were warriors in their minds and hearts first, long before that fact manifested itself in their actions.

As a Mighty Man of Valor, you must learn to protect and nurture your thoughts. It starts small, innocently enough, passing through your mind like a faint light in the distance. You devote no energy to it. Besides, it was just a thought — you would never take action. The next time, it stays in your mind a bit longer, you think about it a little more, dwell on it a little while longer. Time goes by and it's back again. It's no longer just a thought, but now a daydream. You find yourself in bed thinking of how life would be if it were real. You can't stand it anymore. You now think about it all the time, it's consuming you, you must act. But you realize this one time isn't enough to satisfy you. So you relent again. . . and again. You cannot stop now even if you wanted to. Now you're trapped! You know you should stop but your thoughts have become actions. They are now so very real. You continue to move forward, giving in until you no longer care. You justify and rationalize. You start telling yourself that this OK and that it's not important. This is when the cover-up begins. Evidence starts to trickle out and you begin to lie in an effort to hide your actions. Now you're stuck! You cannot give in to your conscience because you still fear who you might hurt if they found out. You are now a prisoner of your own desires. A day comes when you just cannot take it anymore. Your mind is being overwhelmed by the deception and you come to realize that your life is not really yours at all.

No one can change the way you think about something or what you think about, you must do it for yourself. You must be the one to take responsibility for what you're thinking. Many times we take the line that what is happening around us is outside our control. After all how can we possibly have a good day and control our thoughts when the wife is cranky and the kids are out of their minds? Maybe the boss is piling the work on and the grass is now three feet high. The gutters need cleaning and the car needs its oil changed as well. Oh! And don't forget that the taxes are due on Monday! The answer lies in knowing that it doesn't matter what other people do. It is our interpretation of the situation that gets us upset, not the situation itself. Accept what it is and move on. Learn to what you are saying to yourself. Are you saying positive things about yourself or are you concentrating on all the little tasks that you didn't complete? The first step in overcoming a negative thought process is recognizing that there is one. Once you are there you can begin to replace them with something a bit more positive. You must learn to become mentally tough by realizing that the longest journey you will take will be the one between your ears. Napoleon once said, *"There are but two powers in the world, the sword and the mind. In the long run the sword is always beaten by the mind."* Mighty men wear armor around our minds much in the same way we wear it on our bodies. Each and every day we don it knowing that if we don't we enter the battlefield completely defenseless before an enemy that will do everything in its power to overwhelm us. But we know even the armor itself may not be enough. We know our bodies and minds must be made to be as strong as the armor we wear. This is accomplished in much the same way you would strengthen your physical muscles exercising them over and over until the results have been achieved.

Here are five tips for developing mental toughness:

Realize that Thought always involves risk.
Every direction that you move in your thought life will bring with it some element of challenge and risk of error and determining the level at which you are willing to absorb will benefit you immensely. It's what the corporate analysts call 'risk appetite.' Risks need to be considered in terms of both opportunities and threats and may not be confined to any one area such as money. The level at which you are willing to take risks will differ depending on strength of your thoughts. For instance, when you have money, you will find yourself much more willing to sacrifice some because the reason you have it in the first place is because you thought differently in a particular situation. You know that you can always get more. When you are low on funds you find yourself much less willing to give any up on a less-than-sure thing because in your mind the source is limited. Your willingness to take a few risks will invariably impact your performance and reputation but it all starts with the way you think. It is about taking well considered risks where the long-term rewards are expected to be greater than any short-term losses.
How you think about a particular subject will affect how and to what

degree you influence that particular subject. I am a hard-core, right-wing, conservative Republican because of the way I think about certain issues in the political and moral realms. Based on those thoughts, I make decisions that hopefully will propel me forward in doing what I can to act on the issues I deem important. My liberal, Democratic friends, who are great people but view things differently than me and feel the need to constantly question my standards and beliefs. They want to know why I think the way I do because they don't think the same way. This can be somewhat daunting to others because they feel they do not want to cause an argument which might lead to bad feelings between them and their friends. That is the risk you take. I personally would rather be left with someone respecting me even if we cannot agree on a subject because I know I will have a greater influence on the way they think in the long term. People, in general, are reticent to taking action, for fear of offending someone or causing some sort of rift in their relationship. Inaction is always worse than wrong action. In the military, doubt kills people. In the business world, doubt can destroy an opportunity before it ever gets off the ground. Let's say you want to start your own business. I think everyone, at some point, has the dream of becoming an entrepreneur within them. The realization that successful business ownership isn't easy or quick is a great start, but actually understanding the traits and skills necessary can be a bit trickier. All successful entrepreneurs are risk takers in that they weigh every decision before moving forward. The point is they move forward. They know that risk taking is an inherent part of business ownership, because staying 'safe' rarely pays off and they will need the help and support of different people in order to pull off their ideas. They know that waiting for everything to fall into place or to be exactly right is a recipe for failure. They are also aware that nothing will drive people from you faster than your inability to make a decision and since decisions are based upon thoughts, you are declaring your inability to think. Realize that most decisions require some degree of risk and thought beforehand but don't be afraid to do something even if that something is a bit scary. Also never doubt or question the decision once it is made. You can always adjust later if necessary but always move forward.

Understand the Battle of the Mind.

Everyone out there wants a piece of your mind. Relatives want a piece. Co-workers want a piece. Retailers would like a big piece, hence the constant onslaught of commercials all vying for your attention. There is a very real battle going on inside your head and you have the power to determine who will win. You are the focus of relentless efforts to alter your beliefs. Do you think Hollywood is concerned about improving your mental and moral health? Do you think that constantly watching scenes of violence and sex has no negative effect on your mind? I personally know more people who log more time watching TV than they do any other activity including sleep. I had a friend once who admitted to me that he spent just as much time playing video games as he did working, and he worked more than the normal 40-hour week! The bottom line is that TV and movies affect our minds. So do the things we read for that matter. Viewing illicit, electronic media sex and violent programming desensitizes our minds to the things we know are important in our lives. What we feed our minds becomes our thoughts. In Sun Tzu's Art of War, the author makes a statement that we as Mighty Men should all take to heart. "Know thy enemy." The ancient Chinese philosopher was referring to the enemy before you but I think we can take it one step further and add "Know the enemy *within you.*" the quality of your thoughts will determine the quality of your life.

Changing the way you think can be either the most challenging undertaking one can try or it can be the easiest. The answer to the level of difficulty lies within the problem itself. You have to ask yourself "am I willing to change my thoughts?" You notice I didn't ask if you were able but rather I asked if you are willing. All of us are able to change the way we think about things but the real challenge lies in whether we are willing to or not. This is the question that must be answered and it must be done so before we enter the arena. Remember my liberal, Democratic friends? Over the years, we have debated almost every subject known to man. Even when presented with clear, concise, indisputable facts they are unwilling to change the way they think about certain issues. At this point, in my opinion, they are just being hard-headed. It becomes a conscious choice to NOT change the way they think. Knowing what you believe and why you believe will strengthen and solidify your confidence and allow you to be more aware going into the battle better prepared to fight. Having this taken care of beforehand will help you stay focused, stay positive, and never give up! Any good military general will tell you that advance intelligence about the enemy can help you to achieve a greater chance of victory on any field of battle but that same advance intelligence about yourself will guarantee it.

Observe the Crowd and Do (Think) the Opposite
Insanity has been defined as doing the same thing again and again and expecting a different result. It's sort of like beating your head against a wall and wondering why you constantly have a headache. Have you ever seen someone pulled over on the side of the road, obviously having car trouble but you just kept driving along with all the other cars speeding by the stranded motorist? We tend to assume someone else will respond and take action first, or we might think that our help is not really needed. We debate with ourselves on the merits of stopping and helping or continuing on our way. A lot of the time we make the same decisions over and over, always wondering why afterwards we feel the way we do. We feel guilty for not stopping and helping all the while hoping someone in the crowd stopped to help.

There is a major difference between those who play at being Mighty Men and those who truly are. Look around at any group of people in our society. You will find people who do things because those around them do them. They think the way they do because those around them think that way also. There are people who smoke because their friends smoke and people who drink because they don't want to be left out when their co-workers go out after work. If you ever want to decide why you are the way you are, just look around at your friends and the people you associate with. There are some who engage in activities they know are wrong but don't want to be seen as 'party pooper' to their associates or don't want to change their behavior because the path they have chosen is easier. They believe it's easier to fit in than it is to stand out. You can even find it in professional arenas and it can work in the opposite direction as well. I cannot tell you how many people I have met who have passed on great business opportunities because their family members or friends didn't see the value of the opportunity themselves. They had a 'wait and see' attitude or wanted someone else to test the waters first to see how well it went before they themselves committed but all the while the opportunity was passing them by.

When it comes to making important decisions, you have to place yourself in the driver's seat. You must develop the mindset that life doesn't happen to you, you happen to life. In order to be someone different than you are now, you must decide who you want to be and then find people who are like that. Let's say your desire is to be a better husband; the answer is to find groups or individuals who, as the Bible states, have "fruit on the vine." You can identify these individuals by their wives who most likely display a marked contrast in attitude to everyone around them. A happy wife usually means that there is a loving husband somewhere close by. If you want to be more character-oriented or improve your integrity you must make a point to place yourself near people of character and integrity and see how they act. Pay particular attention to the differences that separate them from the masses. Pick up some pointers. Listen to their conversations. Listen to not only what they say, but observe their attitude when they say it. Do they speak with gladness or sadness in their voice? Do they say or do it with confidence or trepidation? Find out what books they are reading and what activities they engage themselves in. Find out what kind of hobbies they have or what sort of recreational activities they participate in, and then evaluate their results to see if their chosen direction is your chosen direction. If it is then do what they do. If it's not then … well you get the picture.

Society at large is comprised of three kinds of people; those who make things happen, those who watch things happen, and those who wonder what happened. The difference between them is their perspective or how they think. Some are playing to win and some are playing to merely survive. Another major difference between them is the crowd they choose to associate themselves with. The bottom line is the way you live your life is defined by those around you. This doesn't mean that your level of success in any given endeavor is always defined by the people who are engaged in it with you. In only means that you will be affected by the actions they take and the thoughts they have. Your mind will take on the characteristics of the people you are around and the environment you are in, so if you are anxious to improve or change your circumstances you must change what is going into your mind or risk having it and your life remain the same. Earl Nightingale, the legendary speaker and educator, once said, *"If you want to be successful in life, simply watch what most people would do in a given situation, and then do the total opposite--nine times out of ten, you'll receive greater rewards."*

There is a saying that one bad apple can spoil the whole barrel. In more modern terms, one negative person can affect everyone they come into contact with. Have you ever shared your dreams and goals with someone and gotten a less-than-positive response? Have you ever felt emotionally drained after having a conversation with someone? Often you will find that when you share your passion with people, they see everything through their own lens, from their own perspective, and ultimately from their own limiting beliefs. From time to time we have to realize that the people in our lives will not be as enthusiastic about our plans to move forward as we might be. They are sometimes called dream stealers or energy vampires. This doesn't make them bad people but we need to protect those dreams and goals even if it means shielding them from those we hold dear for a brief period of time. There will be times in your life when some of the people around you may become a bit toxic to you. You will find that they complain a lot, they whine, their attitudes are poor and they act helpless. They have a virtual wall of resistance around them. Their desire to want to help you in your chosen endeavor is all but nonexistent. They would rather have a big pity party, blame others and continue to be the victim. There is nothing wrong with having challenges once in awhile, however no one is obligated to be on the receiving end of someone else's negativity all the time. I believe in helping people as all leaders should but I also believe that people need to help themselves first. If they choose not to then it is time to limit your association with them.

Take a chance on something different today. Be courageous enough to do the opposite of what everyone else is doing! I know this might sound crazy or even scary, but think about it with me for a moment. If you want to move forward in the important areas of your life, it actually makes sense to do the opposite of those who are not moving forward. If they are not going where you want to go why would you follow them?

Here's an idea:
When facing a significant challenge in your life, and you feel like blaming a work associate, neighbor, friend, or spouse for some problem in your

life, choose to do the opposite of what almost everyone around you does and accept responsibility. Think of someone you trust and ask yourself "what would they do?" Whenever you share your dreams and ask for feedback, consider the source. Ask yourself; is their response objective or critical? Whichever answer you come up with, try to determine why. Does the person have any experience in the matter? Do they have my best interest in mind? Are they honestly concerned for my well-being? It is inevitable that some people around you may not understand what you are trying to accomplish. They may even become a bit jealous or worse yet they are afraid if you become successful, you will leave them behind. Don't ever allow other people to determine your chances of success. What seems impossible for them may very well be within your reach, especially if it is something you are passionate about. If I listened to everyone all the time you would not be reading this book right now. I would have never joined the Army when I was 17. I would never have made the decision to move to the East Coast and probably would have never met the woman (I like the way you think, though!) of my dreams had I listened to those around me. I had to come to a point where I had to decide which of my friend's opinions I was going to place value on. I had to decide who was positive and encouraging and who was negative and draining. Limiting your associations doesn't mean you stop loving them, but rather you make a mental decision as to whether or not to spend time with them. You need to continually monitor the affect of the people around you. Sometimes you need to reduce the time you spend with some in your life in order to expand your network and make room for new people. And sometimes the only way to strengthen a relationship is to take a break from it.

Your physical time and emotional energy are two of your most precious resources. You must make a point of getting around positive people who want to help you achieve your dreams and have you help them with theirs. It's called the Mastermind Alliance and was first defined by Napoleon Hill in his book "Think and Grow Rich." A mastermind, by Hill's definition, is a *"coordination of knowledge and effort, in a spirit of harmony, between two or more people for the attainment of a definite purpose."* Hill further states, *"Economic advantages may be created by any person who surrounds himself with the advice, counsel and personal co-operation of a group of men or women who are willing to lend him wholehearted aid, in a spirit of perfect harmony. This form of co-operative alliance has been the basis of nearly every great fortune. Your understanding of this great truth may definitely determine your financial status."* The most productive people in your life will be the ones who read, who have a hunger to learn, to grow, and they enjoy making positive contributions to the lives of others. In short, they are the ones who think [and act] the way you do.

Ever felt like giving up on your goals because the journey is challenging? Don't let that happen! Do the opposite of what the majority of people do and say to yourself, "No matter how hard it is or how bad it gets, I'm going to keep going." Refuse to quit! Does the idea of standing in front of a crowd of people and speaking in public scare you out of your wits? Then do the opposite, stand up and be heard. Do you find yourself talking too much? Then again, do the opposite. Be quiet and listen (I know a few people reading this who I hope will take it to heart). I think you get the point. Do it for yourself, not everyone else. At the end of the day when all is said and done you are the one that has to live with the decision so why not make one that is best for you.

Learn to Separate Emotion from Thought.
Mighty Men play their emotions close to the vest. They don't hang them out where everyone can be affected by them. They know that emotions are unconscious reactions to stimuli which take more energy to maintain and thoughts are conscious reactions. Take, for instance, a guy who punches another; the guy who received the punch is more likely to be mad for a brief period of time, but the sadness that is incurred might last for a much longer time. Whereas the guy who threw the punch will only be mad for a second. Once the punch has been delivered, his thoughts will take him on to something else (most likely a defense for the punch he knows is coming back in his direction). The guy who delivered the punch is emotional briefly, then thoughtful whereas the recipient of the punch becomes emotional and stays that way because his emotions operate on an unconscious level.

So what's the point here? If someone punches you, before you fly off the handle and start raining your own blows down on them, stop and think for a moment. Make a mental effort to kick your thought into gear and ask yourself, "why are they punching me" Was it in jest or did something happen that can be rectified in way besides a full scale war? This same principle can apply to someone who says something derogatory to you or does something behind your back that will cause you grief and pain. They might even do something right to your face that will in some way cause you heartache. The more you make the effort to think before you act in your own challenges the easier it will be to make this a habit so when someone comes to you emotionally distraught about something in their own life, you will not be overwhelmed by their emotions and begin to have reactions based upon them. Rather, because of the habits you have developed you can deal with the situation in a logical and thoughtful manner that will most likely solve the problem instead of exacerbating it further.

I have a great mentor, Larry, who once made the statement "If it will not matter five years from now then it most likely doesn't matter now." This is the first thing I ask myself when a crisis arrives and must be dealt with. It has helped tremendously because it helps me focus my thoughts on the solution and not my reactions. Are you going through a difficult time right now? Perhaps the promotion you were expecting didn't come through or a friend has betrayed you. Maybe your son just wrecked the car and it was his fault. Maybe you were just told by the doctor that they need to do further tests because something isn't quite right. The easy path, the one chosen by lesser men is to become negative and bitter. When we face difficult times, we can respond in one of two ways. We can look for answers and allow these experiences to strengthen and build our character; or we can withdraw, hold a grudge, become angry or seek revenge which only weakens us in the long run. The question we have to ask ourselves is; which way is more productive? Whatever challenge you're facing, whatever adversity is before you, use it to become a stronger person. Look at it as an object lesson from which you can obtain some new experience or knowledge that may help someone else. Whatever you're going through, be strong and courageous. Always be careful to guard yourself against the negative counterproductive emotions.

Years ago in their "Science of Success" course, W. Clement Stone and Napoleon Hill told the story of Milo C. Jones that I believe illustrates the power of your thoughts and what can be accomplished when that power is harnessed. Milo C. Jones, a farmer from Wisconsin, was stricken down with paralysis a few years ago. So bad was the stroke that he could not turn himself in bed or move a muscle of his body. His physical body was useless, but there was nothing wrong with his brain, so it began to function in earnest, probably for the first time in its existence. Before the stroke, Mr. Jones seemed unable to make his farm yield more than the bare necessities of life. His relatives put him to bed believing him to be a helpless invalid.

For weeks he remained unable to move a single muscle. All he had left was his mind, the one great power he had upon so rarely because he had earned his living by the use of his brawn. Lying flat on his back in bed, Mr. Jones made that brain create a new definite purpose. That purpose was something that he had never known before. His new definite purpose was to make pork sausage.

Calling his family around him he told of his plans and began directing them in carrying the plans into action. He told them: "I can no longer work with my hands so I have decided to work with my mind. The rest of you will have to take the place of my hands" With nothing to aid him except a sound mind and plenty of self-confidence, Milo C. Jones spread the name and reputation of "Little Pig Sausage" all over the United States, and accumulated a fortune besides. Where thought prevails power may be found!

Your mind is a powerful tool that when harnessed can create a different reality. It is physically and mentally impossible for you to conceive anything beyond the limits of your own mind. Through thoughts you give direction to your words and actions. You can choose your focus and how you invest your energy, which gives you the power to design your life to be whatever you choose in each and every moment.

The US Army leadership manual defines a thought process that all Mighty Men should strive to adhere to. It is based upon a BE-KNOW-DO framework which states that leaders should always BE the leader first in their own minds. They should always have some mental picture of the kind of leader they want to be. Knowing how this may be accomplished and actually taking the steps to do what is necessary are both great guidelines but it all must start with the BE because ultimately leadership is more about "being" than about "doing." Mighty Men of Valor know that leadership isn't about position, it's about influence and in order to lead others you must make sure you are being as much of an influence in your own house as possible first. This means that in your own mind, right now, you must be mentally capable of being a Mighty Man. The actual results will come later but not without first establishing what principles are necessary in order to guide our behavior.

Chapter 7
Mighty Men Build and Define Their Lives

"The quality of an individual is reflected in the standards they set for themselves." Ray Kroc - Founder of McDonald's

In 1907, Lord Robert Baden-Powell, a Lieutenant General in the British Army, formed what we know of today as the Boy Scouts. He started this organization with the stated aim of supporting young boys in their physical, mental, and spiritual development, so that they may eventually have constructive roles in society. In 2007, this organization (Boy Scouts and Girl Scouts) had grown to over 38 million members in 216 countries.

In my youth I had the honor and privilege of joining the ranks of the Boy Scouts and eventually receiving the highest award in Scouting, the rank of an Eagle Scout. The Scouting program is one of the finest character building programs available today outside Bible study and application or the military. Its statutes of conduct form the ideal framework for a person striving to become a Mighty Man of Valor. The Scout Law was designed as a guideline and example for Scouts to live their lives. It states that a Scout shall be:

1. Trustworthy
2. Loyal
3. Helpful
4. Friendly
5. Courteous
6. Kind
7. Obedient
8. Cheerful
9. Thrifty
10. Brave
11. Clean
12. Reverent

When writing Scouting for Boys, General Baden-Powell drew inspiration from the work of Ernest Thompson Seton, who founded the Woodcraft Indians in 1902 and later became instrumental in spreading Scouting throughout North America. Baden-Powell also drew inspiration for the Scout Law from the Bushido code of the Japanese Samurai, laws of honor of the American Indians, the code of chivalry for European knights, and the Zulu fighters he had fought against during his military career.

Trustworthy
A Mighty Man tells the truth. He is honest, and keeps his promises. People can depend on him. Being "worthy of trust" means a promise made is a promise kept. If you tell someone you will do something, you are honor-bound to carry out that promise to the very best of your ability, and to let nothing interfere with your completing it. You are trustworthy, not because you are forced to be, but rather because you choose to be. If you were to willfully break this promise by telling a lie, or by not carrying out the promise, you know you will lose the right to make any more such promises and also lose the privilege of having people follow you as their leader. You are punctual, prompt, and able to persevere. A trustworthy man realizes that the simple commitments are every bit as important as the difficult ones. He knows that trust is earned, not given, and is always looking to strengthen that relationship.

Loyal
The family, friends, leaders, and nation of a Mighty Man of Valor know that he will stick to them through thick and thin against any who would threaten them, either physically or verbally. He always remains steady in his adherence to what is right. People know that he will stand for what is right even when no one is watching. He knows that true loyalty is given when nothing is personally gained. A Mighty Man is loyal to his own leaders and supports them in their decisions. He is loyal to the laws of his country and the people who make, enforce, and interpret those laws; he may disagree but he always shows respect for authority. He knows sometimes he may lose friends, loves, and even popularity by being truthful but he will never lose his honor.

Helpful
A Mighty Man cares about other people. He is a servant leader contributing to the welfare of others and willfully volunteers to help others without expecting payment or reward. He always tries to put others first, knowing it may place his own needs in jeopardy. He is always ready,

willing, and able to help and is constantly observing the world around him so he is prepared to act if needed. It is nothing for him to give up his own pleasure, comfort, or safety to perform his duty. When faced with difficulty, he always asks himself two questions, "What is my duty?" and "What is best for other people?" A Mighty Man is always prepared to answer those questions to the fullest and be the example no matter the consequences.

Friendly

A Mighty Man of Valor is a friend to all. He is a brother and comrade to other Mighty Men and offers friendship and help to all who would ask it. He tries to be friendly to everyone he meets, giving them the benefit of the doubt until their character becomes apparent. He realizes his friendship may be taken, rejected, or lost completely on people. A Mighty Man has the ability to see a person's value beyond social standing and knows to accept people based on their words and actions. He realizes that not all their beliefs and customs will be the same as his, but he never ridicules anyone for them. He loves the sinner but hates the sin. A Mighty Man accepts the other man as he finds him and makes the best of him, always being the example so that the other may better himself or change should he so choose. When he meets someone of poor character, he continues to be friendly to him in the hope that his example may influence the other man to change his behavior; however, he realizes he must limit his friendship with such flawed persons lest he be seen as associating too closely with them. A Mighty Man can, in a friendly manner, refuse to join in any activities or behaviors that may be considered to be of questionable character.

Courteous

A Mighty Man is a gentleman. He treats his wife like the queen he wants her to be and his children like the future leaders he knows they can be. He knows that being courteous is a product of having respect for other people and believes that being courteous without the intention of determining respect for the person is a lie. He knows he must treat everyone the same until he is given a reason to do otherwise. He cannot be courteous and friendly to those of high social and professional station and at the same time treat lesser ranked people with ridicule. He knows that all people are important and deserve his time, attention, and appreciation.

Kind

A Mighty Man knows there is strength in being gentle. He follows the Golden rule and treats others as he would like to be treated. He always keeps his passions and emotions in check. He knows that the first place he must practice kindness is in his own home. A Mighty Man will always maintain a gentle attitude and even when provoked will refuse to set aside his honor or character to exchange insults. He knows that others may have different views and will try to understand them through discernment and compassion. If his own views are called into question he always tries to portray those views in such a way that the other person will be educated, not attacked.

Obedient

A Mighty Man of Valor follows the rules of God, Country, and Family. He obeys the laws of his community and organization, always being the example that others may duplicate. He is disciplined emotionally, physically, and spiritually, placing his relationship with God first. He constantly seeks to strengthen that relationship through obedient spiritual behavior. If he thinks the rules are unfair, he attempts to change them rather than disobey them. A Mighty Man does not blindly do what he is told but he does have the discipline to do his duty. He knows his duty is to support the goals of his organization even though he may not fully understand them. He is mature enough to know the difference between being independent and being free of responsibility. He has enough self-discipline to be obedient to his conscience, which may not be the easiest task but his honor will insist it be done.

Cheerful

A Mighty Man knows that the only things he can control are his attitude and his actions. He cheerfully performs the tasks sets before him. He never whines, grumbles, complains, criticizes, or wallows in self-pity, but rather chooses to get the job done and do it with energetic purpose. To him complaining is the refuge for those who have developed no self-confidence. He knows that the average person does what they do for money or fame but a Mighty Man does what he needs to do for a purpose or cause. He never complains of hardships but instead works to improve, even under the most annoying circumstances. His cheerful words are always a reflection of his cheerful thoughts. His lives by the principle that problems should be dealt with in private and praise should be aired in public. A Mighty Man knows that a spirit of cheerfulness requires that he understand life and all the blessings contained within it. He is aware that a certain amount of hardship is required in order to test his character and therefore his ability to be cheerful. He is constantly challenged to find ways of teaching others to be happy. He asks God everyday not to remove the challenges but for Him to give him the strength to overcome and learn from them.

Brave
A Mighty Man will face danger even though he may be afraid. He has the courage to stand for what he knows is right even though others may laugh at him or threaten him. He knows fear will come in many forms; fear of failure, fear of the unknown, fear of looking foolish or stupid, all of which will cause him to develop bad habits. He knows that the habits of making excuses or blaming others are formed by fear. He always attempts, when necessary, to accept the blame and apologize for mistakes. He knows that bravery comes in many shapes and sizes and that without fear there is no need for bravery. A Mighty Man knows that when he experiences fear he has two choices: He can control the fear or it can control him. He never loses himself to the idea of self over others. He knows he must train himself to meet that feeling with courage rather than cowardice. He knows fear will give him strength and will allow him to focus on getting the job done. He must look for every opportunity to defend the weak, the truth, and his honor. He is always willing to put the needs of others ahead of his own even though it may be uncomfortable or unprofitable.

Clean
A Mighty Man keeps his body, mind, and spirit fit and clean. He chooses the company of those who live by his same high standards. He knows that cleaning dirt from his skin is a simple thing but that it is a much more difficult task to clean filthy thoughts, habits, and behaviors from his life. He knows that associating with others who demonstrate clean minds and mouths is the best way for him to remain clean. A Mighty Man knows that encouragement, praise, and support are strong detergents to the stains in people's lives. He is aware that lying, stealing, and cheating are all habits formed in an unclean mind. He refrains from dirty jokes, vulgar comments, ridicule, and racial slurs because he knows that they are more

likely to diminish his character. He makes every attempt to change the behavior of the group by making his feelings known and then removing himself from the group rather than continually allowing the group to bombard him with their dishonorable actions and statements.

Reverent
A Mighty Man of Valor is faithful to God. He is dutiful and faithful in his beliefs and the responsibilities that come with those beliefs. He knows that respecting the beliefs of others can be a challenge, especially when they conflict with his own. He doesn't ridicule them for their beliefs but rather attempts to engage them in healthy constructive dialog which allows him to educate them on his own beliefs as well has himself to theirs. He strives to give others the freedom to believe what they may have found to be true in their lives but doesn't allow it or them to affect his own beliefs and convictions. A Mighty Man remains true to the truth.

Many of you may not have had the opportunity to be a Boy Scout but that doesn't mean that you cannot use the examples set by this organization as a guide for your lives. The guidelines set forth in the Scout Law were designed to be used as a road map or a standard of behavior for up-and-coming leaders, but we as Mighty Men of Valor can take advantage of it as well - if we choose to follow it.

Chapter 8
Mighty Men are Righteous

"When the whole world is against you...you must go on doing what you can, fulfilling your duty and, in the end, going down with honor." - Austria-Hungary Emperor Franz Joseph

One of my favorite men in the Bible was Joshua because he embodied every characteristic of a true Mighty Man of Valor. He was the consummate definition of a "man's man." He was smart, courageous, faithful, tough, and even tender when needed. He held together one of the largest volunteer armies in history and never backed down from a fight. Even though he eventually assumed the leadership role over his people, he never tried to usurp Moses' role before his time. He never tried to be Moses but rather found his own style of leadership and was true to himself. Turning and running wasn't an option and never crossed his mind. Joshua was a "whatever it takes" type of leader, having a no-nonsense attitude when it came to his responsibilities. He was by-the-book and out-of-the-box at the same time. He was the kind of man who waited patiently for God's direction then moved unflinchingly forward to accomplish His will. Almost everyone he knew was stubborn and willing to listen at some point; but Joshua was always prepared to risk unpopularity to carry out God's commands. . He knew that all leaders at some point must be willing to take risks and pay whatever price to do what they know to be right.

Joshua was the son of Nun, of the tribe of Ephraim, which was known at the time as the most militaristic of the tribes of Israel, largely because of Joshua's campaigns. Having come from a family and community of warriors, he learned by association and hard work to become one himself. He was born in Egypt during the Israelite enslavement, and shared in all the events of the Exodus. He and his buddy Caleb were the only two adults who remembered the Egyptian captivity and lived to see their people delivered to the Promised Land. He was also one of the twelve spies who were sent in by Moses to explore the land of Canaan, and only he and Caleb believed enough to be willing to overcome the enemies and therefore gave an encouraging report. Moses was his mentor and accompanied him part of the way when he ascended Mount Sinai to receive the Ten Commandments. He was appointed overall military command of the Israelite army at their first battle against the Amalekites in which he was victorious.

Joshua was appointed by Moses to succeed him as leader of the Israelite nation upon his death. He commanded the subsequent conquest of Canaan and their first major conflict was in Jericho, a heavily fortified city just five miles west of the Jordan River, northwest of the Dead Sea. He and the Israelites took Jericho by following God's instruction in which he ordered the host to march around the city for seven days, whereupon the city walls fell, just as God said they would. Jericho was one of the oldest continuously-inhabited and heavily defended cities in the world. When it fell, the Israelites slaughtered "every living thing" inside Jericho and completely destroyed the city except for Rahab and her family, who had aided the two spies sent by Joshua to check out the city.

One of his first moral and political challenges came when Achan, a common foot soldier, violated a rule God had set forth about taking any of the spoils. He disobeyed and took some garments and silver he found in the city, hiding them in his tent. As a result of this defiance, when Joshua sent a small force out to conquer Ai, a small neighboring city just west of Jericho, they were defeated and 36 Israelite warriors were killed. Joshua immediately sensed something was wrong. There was no reason why they should have not been able to conquer Ai. He sought God's guidance and eventually identified Achan as the reason for their defeat. Achan's sin was exposed and he, his entire family, their possessions, and his animals were all destroyed per Joshua's orders.

After defeating the inhabitants of Ai, the Israelites then faced an alliance of the remaining kings at Gibeon. Following the destruction of Jericho and Ai, the people of Gibeon sent ambassadors to trick Joshua and the Israelites into making a treaty with them. According to the Bible, the Israelites were commanded to destroy ALL the inhabitants of Canaan. The Gibeonites presented themselves as ambassadors from a distant land and, without consulting the high priests, Israel entered into a non-aggression agreement with them. Joshua realized he been deceived, and kept his word with the Gibeonites to let them live, but cursed and enslaved them as woodcutters and water-carriers. The Five Kings of the Amorites (the kings of Hebron, Jarmuth, Lachish, Eglon, and Jerusalem), besieged the

Gibeonites, whom they perceived as traitors. They rushed to Joshua seeking his help; his response was to launch a surprise attack following a night march, causing the Amorites to panic and flee. Joshua defeated them because God caused the sun and moon to stand still so that they could finish the battle in daylight. After the five kings' cowardly attempt at avoiding retribution by hiding inside a cave, they were discovered and trapped there until their army had been completely obliterated. After their defeat, the kings were brought to Joshua, who first humiliated them, then ordered their death and had them impaled for public display. At sunset, the bodies were thrown back into the cave in which they had hidden, and the entrance sealed.

Joshua then switched roles, going from overall military commander to what amounted to national president. He shifted his focus from command to govern. After dividing the conquered lands amongst the tribes, Joshua led them to their Promised Land and then spent his time and resources admonishing them to be loyal to their God, whose power and love had been so mightily manifested through their trials. Soon afterward he died, at the age of 110.

Joshua was strong and courageous. When the fight came to him he was always ready and willing. When he was instructed to take the fight to his enemies he never once questioned its purpose or necessity. He helped the Israelites defeat their enemies several times by the might of his sword and the power of his faith in God. When the attack started he was out in front, not directing it from some rearward position. He didn't stand around offering advice from his vast repository of experience and knowledge. He went out and showed people how it was done. A man of such great valor could easily become prideful, especially since the people loved him without question [most of the time], yet we notice he was willing to listen to what God would have him do and wasn't afraid to stand up before his people and relay those instructions. He was regularly and totally in submission to God which is something we as Mighty Men can take to heart. We need to stay focused on what God wants for His people not what the people may want for themselves. Peer pressure can break a leader who is not locked into his relationship with the Lord. Spiritual leaders do not necessarily go along with the majority but rather follow the instructions of their sovereign God.

Being a man of God and a Mighty Man of Valor we, too, can follow the footsteps of this wonderful leader and learn from his trials and victories. From his life we can learn what it means to be a Mighty Man of Valor and apply it to our own lives.

He knew what was right
I am sure that Joshua faced a bit of criticism when he announced that the people were to march around the city of Jericho day after day. One can almost picture the scene: It's unbearably hot and dusty and you and your friends have done nothing for the past few days but march round and round some stupid pile of rocks surrounded by thick high walls. All the while, the inhabitants of the city have been yelling obscenities and making fun of you. And the worst part has been you have been doing it fully armored. I would be a bit irritated too. Joshua wasn't perturbed by any of it because he was doing what he knew God wanted him to do. I am sure it came down to whether he wanted the people mad at him or God disappointed in him. When you view it through that prism, the choice is always easy, making it simple to stand up to any negative responses that may come your way. Consider the leadership style differences between Joshua and Moses. One was a diplomat, while the other was an in-your-face military commander. Moses patiently listened to the people's complaints whereas Joshua confronted them head-on. Both taught the people what was right but did it in different ways.

The notorious American Wild West bank robber Jesse James was hunted by the authorities, but was held in high regard by many ordinary folk. Here's an example of why: A story goes that Jesse James and his gang had taken refuge for a few days in a ramshackle farmhouse after one of their raids. The old widow who lived there fed the men, and apologized for her modest offerings and the poor state of the accommodation. While the gang lay low, they learned from the widow that she faced eviction from her landlord and was expecting a visit from his debt collector any day. When it came time for them to leave, they took pity on the old lady and gave her several hundred dollars, a small fortune in those days, to settle her debt. The gang moved on, but only to a nearby copse, where for a couple more days they watched and waited for the arrival, and departure, of the debt collector -- whom they promptly held up and robbed.

Obviously, the story is amusing but that doesn't make it right. So many times I see parents taking their children to see what have been billed as funny animated movies but are really adult shows filled with adult humor. Just because the feature is a cartoon or is billed as child-friendly does not necessarily make it proper for your kids' moral development. Hollywood puts out movies today that adults shouldn't be watching, let alone children, but every month millions upon millions of parents shell out hundreds of millions of dollars only to expose their children to rubbish that erodes their moral values. As the leader of your family you must know what is right so that when trials present themselves you will know how to act on them.

He had the courage to do what was right
When Achan was found guilty of hoarding treasure from the Battle of Jericho, Joshua had a dilemma. The Israelites had failed to take Ai because one of their number had failed to live by the rules. God told them to not take any spoils when they sacked Jericho but Achan saw the wealth of the Canaanites and was tempted to sin. All Achan had to do was quickly confess and repudiate the sin when it happened. Instead he chose to follow the dictates of his heart, knowing full well that it was wrong. He tried to hide the sin but soon found out that which is thought of in secret will soon become open for all to see. The story illustrates a point that we as leaders, from time to time, may have to remove someone who stands in the way of the work. When someone compromises the values of your organization it is up to you to make it right before the ripple effect hurts other people.

Joshua knew there had to be a reason this little podunk town in the middle of nowhere that couldn't even afford a third letter in their name was able to resist them. He went and asked God why they were unable to overcome such an insignificant foe, to which He told Joshua of the sin. Joshua ordered everyone's belongings inspected and Achan was found out. He tried to make an excuse for his sin but it was too late. The lesson here is that our sin affects not only us but those around us as well. The worst enemy that you or I have is ourselves, this enemy occupies the same space that we occupy, he uses the same brain that you and I use to concoct his destructive thoughts, he uses the same hands that you and I use to perform his harmful deeds. That which is inside of us can and will do more damage than any outside force ever will. We are faced with choices almost minute by minute of each and every day. It is how we answer those choices that will determine our status as a Mighty Man.

He was capable of showing others what was right
One of the most famous quotes attributed to Joshua came when he offered the people a choice. They had to decide whether they would follow God or follow the gods of the people around them. God makes it clear that if the nation turned from Him, He would turn against them. Joshua states: *choose you this day whom ye will serve; . . . but as for me and my house, we will serve the Lord" (Josh. 24:2, 15).* Joshua took a stand and set the standard for who he and his family would follow. You as a mighty man must choose today who you are going to serve. Are you going to serve your boss or your family? Will you stand for the values you know are right, or will you knuckle under to peer pressure? Will you make the right choice or the most convenient one? The choice is yours, nobody else can make it for you. To fail to choose is itself a choice, and it is undoubtedly the wrong one!

In 326 BC, Alexander the Great attacked a small city-fortress near the Hydaspes River after marching fifty miles through waterless desert. His men were at the end of their rope, both physically and emotionally. They had been constantly moving and fighting for almost 10 years. Like frightened and desperate troops the world over, they began to fight with savage, almost hysterical cruelty; rape and wholesale massacre became the norm for them.

Twice during the siege his troops refused to mount the scaling-ladders being used to assault the walls, until the king himself led the way, and shamed them into following him. A priest warned Alexander against pressing the attack: the signs indicated danger to his life. Alexander ignored the advice and shouted for the scaling-ladders to be brought up. The men hung back, hesitating; a furious Alexander snatched a ladder himself, leaned it against the top of the wall, and went straight up, holding a light shield over his head as protection. When he reached the top, he quickly cut down the defenders barring his way, and stood alone for a moment atop the battlements - a perfect target for any archer. His friends shouted to him to come back. Instead, with splendid bravado, he jumped down inside the fortress. His back against the wall, he proceeded to take on all comers single-handed. His gesture had the desired effect – his men followed him, more concerned for his safety now than their own. Alexander never asked his men to do anything he himself was unwilling to do. Because of his example, his men were then willing to live a life worthy of his risk in going before them.

One interesting point to note is that nowhere in Scripture is Joshua described as being a man of extraordinary might, talent, or intellect. What made him special was his sense of what was right. Today, there is a whole generation of people who have turned their backs on what is right and haven't looked back. The problem lies in the fact they do not even know that it isn't right. They have grown up with the full weight of worldly influences upon them. It used to be that sex, drugs, and rock-n-roll were things to be avoided, but in today's society they are almost considered requirements. Here is a news flash for some parents: It is not the public school system's responsibility, or society as a whole, to teach your children the difference between right and wrong. It is yours as the parent! If you find that you have not done this, take a stand now and do not back down. It will be hard but it will also be worth it. They will challenge you but in the end they will respect you. You must set the example and the standard for them with your life and your words. You, as the man, must choose to live ahead of your contemporaries and above the circumstances. Are you raising your children in a way that they know what you believe and why you believe it? If you're not, they will follow the same path. They will grow up not knowing what they believe or why they believe it. Lead your family for their sake. Don't shirk your responsibilities or push them off on another. Do the right thing!

Chapter 9
Mighty Men are Mentors

The Bible shows us that Moses was mightily used by God but it also tells us that Moses knew he wouldn't be around forever. He knew God's work would go on long after he was gone and that the people would need someone to guide them. As all leaders should do, he kept his eye out for someone with a heart and spirit capable of leading the children of Israel. He found that man in Joshua.

> Moses said to Joshua, *"Choose us out men, and go out, fight with Amalek: tomorrow I will stand on the top of the hill with the rod of God in mine hand. So Joshua did as Moses had said to him, and fought with Amalek: and Moses, Aaron, and Hur went up to the top of the hill. And it came to pass, when Moses held up his hand, that Israel prevailed: and when he let down his hand, Amalek prevailed. But Moses' hands were heavy; and they took a stone, and put it under him, and he sat thereon; and Aaron and Hur stayed up his hands, the one on the one side, and the other on the other side; and his hands were steady until the going down of the sun. And Joshua discomfited Amalek and his people with the edge of the sword. And the LORD said unto Moses, Write this for a memorial in a book, and rehearse it in the ears of Joshua: for I will utterly put out the remembrance of Amalek from under heaven. And Moses built an altar, and called the name of it Jehovahnissi: For he said, because the LORD hath sworn that the LORD will have war with Amalek from generation to generation."*

It was interesting to see how Moses sent his young protégé' into battle. Although he allowed Joshua to initially fight the battle, he was never far away. He was within sight of Joshua all the time and while he told him what to do, he also let Joshua take the action himself. Moses allowed Joshua to fight and win the battle, but he gave guidance where it was needed.   This is a perfect example of the successful mentoring relationship. Moses demonstrated the wisdom of a mentor by deciding to delegate an important task to Joshua, who in turn did what he was good at: battle command. In taking this action, Moses demonstrated trust in Joshua's gifts and leadership potential. He opened the way for their ongoing mentoring relationship.

We see a pattern forming in the relationship between Moses and Joshua. First, Moses did the work and then allowed Joshua to do the same, while he stood nearby because he knew, eventually, Joshua would do the work after Moses was gone. That's the mentoring pattern for raising a new generation of Mighty Men. First, we do the work. Then, they do the work with us guiding them. Finally they do the work.

Moses probably had many whom he relied upon as leaders but he was always looking for that one individual who stood out from the others. He looked for the one who came early and stayed late or who was always an active participant instead of a spectator. It's an easy thing to train people in the details of a task but it's another thing to train them to train others. Because Moses mentored Joshua, the work he started didn't stop after he was gone. A new generation was prepared to take up the torch and run the race.

Being the head of your house and the lord of your castle endows you with a terrible power that, if left unchecked, can become abusive. The example we set as Mighty Men of Valor will either grace those who follow us or will damn them. When we mentor someone, we are given the opportunity to rub off on them, like wax on a car. In many ways it is like iron sharpening iron; the mentoring relationship works to the benefit of both those involved. There are a number of factors that go into developing the ideal mentoring environment which we shall discuss in detail.

Mentorship is Not about Control

I once had a young man join my organization whom I'll call Brian. Brian came aboard with us because we offered him something that no one else had, the possibility of a deep and purposeful friendship. You see, Brian grew up in a family of eight children and while his parents did a great job in raising him, there just never seemed to be enough time to devote to any one child. All his siblings loved their parents but never really knew them on an emotional level. There were many areas in which Brian didn't trust or respect his parents. So, when Brian met me, he was searching for that deep emotional attachment that only a father can develop with a son. I became an almost instant father figure to him which, to be honest, was not

101

my intention.

Because of the way our organization was structured at the time, I became Brian's mentor in all aspects of our business and through that began to teach him about life as well. I taught in the only way I knew, through example. The problem was that there were so many gaping holes in Brian's knowledge about certain basic aspects of life that I unconsciously took control in an effort to keep him out of any further trouble. For example: Brian had never had a checkbook, therefore never knew how to balance an account. He would get paid and then cash the check at the local bank. A week later he would be out of money and wondering how his bills were going to get paid. He came to me asking for financial advice. I began by telling him each week to deposit his check and then take out a certain amount for spending. I began to teach him to pay himself first and then his bills. Within a few months his bills were paid and finances were under control. He had even started a savings account which was something he had never thought of before. Where the over-control problem began was with me. I began to find all kinds of things wrong with Brian. He was lax in almost every area of his life, whereas I saw myself as somewhat disciplined. He was used to getting up ten minutes before he had to leave for work and I awoke two hours before my appointed time so that I might devote time to preparing for the day and devotions. Brian had a thousand thoughts going through his mind at any given time, whereas I tended to think about one thing at a time until I developed a solution or plan(this can be good or bad). His lack of focus and discipline in the areas that you and I would consider common sense, drove me crazy most of the time.

I began to see it as my personal mission to make Brian conform to my view of what a productive member of society should be. I began to do whatever I could to control Brian's life. The challenge was that Brian didn't want to be controlled. He wanted to be taught. He didn't want me telling him what to do. He needed me to *show* him what to do. After a couple of failed attempts to straighten him out I noticed that a certain level of resentment had built up between us. The great thing about mentoring is that you cannot be one to someone else unless someone else is one to you. I realized one day that I could never remember resenting my own mentor in any way, which led me to begin to wonder what the differences were in the way I was being mentored and how I was mentoring Brian. Once the difference was out in the open I saw where my mistakes lay and immediately began to correct them. I sat Brian down, apologized to him, detailed the problems and my thoughts on the matter and then asked if we might start over. I knew that it truly wasn't a mistake unless I refused to learn from it. I began to create situations where Brian could watch how I dealt with certain situations or what I would say to people in certain environments. I opened my life up to him so that he might see the value in changing and make the decision to do so himself. Over time, Brian saw the value of my actions and began to duplicate my efforts. That was when I truly began to mentor Brian.

Mentoring is more about Listening *then* Doing

The story is told of Franklin Roosevelt, who often endured long receiving lines at the White House. He complained that no one really paid any attention to what was said. One day, during a reception, he decided to try an experiment. To each person who came down the line and shook his hand, he murmured, "I murdered my grandmother this morning." The guests responded with phrases like, "Marvelous! Keep up the good work. We are proud of you. God bless you, sir." It was not till the end of the line, while greeting the ambassador from Bolivia, that his words were actually heard. Nonplussed, the ambassador leaned over and whispered, "I'm sure she had it coming."

I once read an article that stated married couples only really fight about two things: communication and money. There are so many resources out in the world today concerning improved communication between couples that one wonders why there is such a challenge. My personal perspective is that is not really a communication problem but rather a focus problem. Most people tend to only focus on one thing at a time, so if your spouse is speaking to you while the kids are screaming and the TV is blaring, two of the three have to take a backseat. The other day I was watching my favorite television program and Lisa asked me a question from the dining room. She had been searching for something on the Internet and wanted my opinion on it. I was so into my program that I honestly didn't hear her the first time she asked the question. When she asked it again I was annoyed that she was interrupting my favorite program and only half listened to her question. No one likes to repeat themselves and so when Lisa found herself asking a third time, her personal annoyance meter was off the chart. I realized that my priorities were out of sync which was affecting my ability to focus. No TV program is worth having your wife mad at you!

As men, we need to learn that the opportunities to mentor people will not always come from the people in our business organizations or social spheres of influence. They will start in our very own homes. We have a responsibility to be mentors to our wives and our children. As Dads we must learn to model the behavior we want our children to adopt. Do things like opening the door for Mom once in a while. Go around to her side of the car and open her car door and hold your arm out to help her out of the car; allow her to exit first when leaving an elevator or let her go through the door that you are holding open when leaving or entering your home. In no time at all you will see your children duplicating your actions. You might even watch as your son holds the door for his sister (it can happen!). This behavior will become ingrained in their thought processes until they are second nature, and then you will see them doing it without thinking at all.

It's been said that the average married couple spends 27.5 minutes per week communicating with each other and 46 hours watching television, performing household chores, meeting social obligations, etc. Communication breakdown is an oft-cited culprit in marital problems. If you feel your spouse just doesn't understand you, maybe the problem lies in what you're doing (or what you're not doing).

It may seem funny to you as a reader, but I learned most of my communication tips from watching old westerns when I was kid. It wasn't what the actors said but rather how they said it. They were always slow to speak. They listened before they talked. They would always think about their response before voicing it. They were never hasty and when they did speak they did it in such a way that the other person could understand completely. They always spoke the truth and never ever exaggerated. They never responded in anger unless there was absolutely no other recourse and when they were wrong they admitted it. I used to watch these old shows and, without knowing it, began to develop their habits. In high school I was the guy to go to when someone needed someone else to listen. I really didn't know what to do about most of the problems, but that's not what most people want anyway. They don't want you to solve the problem; they just want someone who will allow them to get the problem out in the open.

Your wife was a gift made to you from the Supreme Commander of the Corps of Mighty Men, and therefore should be given all the attention and respect she deserves. Your responsibility is to provide for her material, spiritual, and emotional needs. This also means making every attempt to listen to her in every situation. Let's say you're with a group of friends and one of them is telling a great story to which you are listening intently. Your wife says something to you from across the room. It may be something as innocent as asking if you know where the car keys are, or it could be to tell you that the building is on fire. There is a choice to be made. Do you stop listening to the person telling the story and risk them thinking you are rude, or do you respect the speaker and put your wife on hold until they are done? In my opinion it comes down who is more deserving of your focus. The speaker's story can always wait. If you explain to them that your wife needs you for a moment and that you would love to hear the end of the story they will respect you more because of your devotion to the one you love. At least they should, and if they don't maybe its time to find a new friend.

Whether it's with your wife or friends, it's annoying and rude when you don't listen. When I say "listen" I mean with your ears *and* your eyes. By not looking directly at the person speaking, you're really telling them that you don't care. Listening is different from hearing in that we are born with the ears to hear, and we use that ability subconsciously, but listening takes focus, energy, time, and practice. One can listen with their heart and mind just as much as they do with their ears. I had a co-worker once named Steve, with whom I differed greatly when it came to political issues. Steve was a staunch liberal whereas I tend to be more hard-line conservative. Steve told me that he really liked debating with me because I was at least was willing to listen to his viewpoint. When I asked him to elaborate, he told me that when he worked at his previous place of employment, he would debate political issues with another co-worker who was, as he put it, of the "right-wing conservative" persuasion. The difference in this instance was that this individual would never listen to Steve's opinion or views. He never wanted to know *why* Steve believed the way he did. Once

Steve opened his mouth on any particular subject he never got another word in because the other individual would capitalize the conversation. So when I met Steve and wanted to know not only what he believed but also why he believed it, it placed the issue in a whole new context. He knew I wasn't just listening with my ears so that I could form my next rebuttal, but also that I was listening with my heart and mind so that I could understand him and see the issue from his perspective. I told Steve the reason I was this way was because I had found from experience that if a person wanders through the woods and finds a path with another person standing on it, it is very difficult to lead them to your destination when you don't know where they were coming from. They may or may not have already come from where you intended to go.

Mentorship is not about Always Having the Answers
It is easy for a mentor to fall into the trap of thinking they have to have all the answers all the time. In a mentoring scenario, dispensing information is often required. It's quick, easy, and may make you feel good about yourself, but more importantly it will answer the question. Before I knew what a mentor was, most men I knew were too proud to ask for help unless there was absolutely no other option. Mentors, business associates, friends and family can all provide valuable insight to assist you in whatever challenge you're facing. I'm sure Moses didn't always have the answers Joshua needed and I am also sure that Joshua didn't expect him to. If you are being mentored by someone, realize that they are not perfect. The husband-wife relationship can be the greatest mentor-mentee exercise of all time. It's about growing together and finding the answers together. Ladies, your husbands will not have all the answers all the time. Don't expect them to. When the gutters overflow or the car starts making strange noises, they may know what to do, but when everything you eat makes you sick and you're rapidly losing weight they may not know why. They will not tell you they don't know why because they don't want you to see the sense of inadequacy they feel at not being able to care for you and protect you. Treat them like the King, not the entire kingdom with its doctors, diplomats, ministers, and magicians and they will rapidly step in to fill that role. They will become your King.

Some ideas you might want to try when you are asked to act as mentor:

Give advice only when you're sure the other person has put some thought into the problem themselves. Once a person has presented me with their particular challenge and I believe I understand the issue at hand, I always try to remember to ask what *they* think they should do. I want to know if they have thought about a solution or if they are merely reacting. I try not to be seen as the "answer guy." When you are always providing the answers, you both run the risk of getting very used to the habit of one always asking and the other answering. The challenge with this habit is that neither of you learn. You as the mentor do not learn to evaluate and coach, and they as the person being mentored are given no opportunity to think for themselves. You can provide direction when they are stuck by asking: "What do you think the solution might be?" or "what options are available to you?" The goal is for them to make the solution their own. Your advice is meant only to get them "unstuck." Don't always jump at the chance to solve the problem before its time. The best solution to any challenge will be the one that the person with the problem came up with because it came from inside and therefore has more impact.

If you find yourself in a position where you are mentoring someone, always make allowances for differences (differences in what?). Develop a concern for the other person's interests. When they see that you are on their side they will be much more prone to open up to you and then the real relationship can begin. Again, learn to listen with your eyes. When they are talking look at them directly, but not right in the eye, as this can be distracting look at the other person's face to see what emotions they may be displaying. You will not only glean copious amounts of information from what they are saying but also from what they are not. Listen to the tone of their voice. Are they angry? Are they concerned? Are they scared or nervous? Are they just relaying facts or are they emotionally attached to the issue somehow? Watch their hands. Are they fidgety or shaking? You can ascertain volumes of information about what's going on just by watching for non-verbal cues.

By allowing you to help them they are letting you know that you are someone they admire and hold in high regard. You, in turn, should return the sentiment. You might be able to help a less experienced person in your field not only answer the same questions you had when you were in their position, you might help them avoid some of the mistakes you made as well. When the person you are mentoring asks questions and causes you think about the answers you give them, it can help you reflect on where you are in your own life and what areas you need to improve upon as well.

Beginning a new mentoring relationship with someone is like trying to grow corn in the Midwest. If it rains too much the corn cannot absorb it all. If it doesn't rain enough the corn starves. The corn needs just the right amount of moisture over the right amount of time in order for it to prosper. And when a storm comes…the corn is better prepared to handle it. When it comes to people if you attempt to do a brain dump on them and impart to them all your accumulated knowledge in as short a time as possible, they will become overwhelmed and eventually quit. If you don't give them enough of your time they will resent you and eventually give up. Biding your time and taking the relationship slowly will produce strong and resilient people who will be much more able to withstand the storms of life and one day become mentors themselves.

Chapter 10
Mighty Men are Made, not Born

"Warriors are not born or mass-produced. Each one has to be hand-crafted, one at a time, by a time-tested process" - Tom Clancy

After Deborah (in the Book of Judges), the Bible says that there was about 40 years of peace in the land of Israel. Then the Israelites started acting up again, and it was during this time that a bunch of hooligans called Midianites started pillaging their homes and lands. It got pretty nasty, pretty fast. In fact, it was recorded that there were so many invaders that they could not be counted. They simply took what they wanted and destroyed everything else. In typical Israelite fashion, they started whining and crying out to God again. This is where Gideon came in.

Gideon was Israel's fourth major Judge after the birth of Joshua. During his tenure, the army of Midian and a couple other nations united against Israel. The Lord told Gideon that he would be made strong and that he was to save Israel from the Midianites. Some commentators portray Gideon's response as one of fright, with Gideon asking the age-old question, "why us?" One would think that this sort of announcement from an angel would shock anyone but in true Mighty Man fashion I believe Gideon went on the offensive. He began to cross examine the Angel of the Lord trying to determine why his people were in the predicament in the first place. Gideon may have been weak in faith, which made it hard for him to reconcile the promises of the Angel with the threat Israel was facing, but it is my belief that Gideon's response was born out of reluctance and frustration.

The Angel answered Gideon's objections and then told him to appear and act as Israel's deliverer. The Angel told Gideon that if he did what he was told the Midianites would be overcome. At first, Gideon didn't put much stock in the Angels prediction; mostly, in my opinion, due to his own perceived lack of skills and position, but God knew that there was more to him than met the eye. He wasn't a leader! He was from a weak clan and the youngest son. He had no experience, so what made the Lord think he would be able to do anything but thresh wheat? These were the thoughts running through Gideon's head and that is exactly where we find Gideon, beating out wheat in order to hide it from the Midianites. Why was he doing this? At minimum it means that he was preparing to protect himself (and likely his family) by thinking ahead enough to be able to keep some of his precious crops. The next thing we notice is that the angel of the Lord referred to Gideon as a "mighty man of valor." Gideon had a quality that made him worthy of honor but he needed to become aware of it. He had the ability to encourage people to be something more than what they were. As far as we know, Gideon had ever been in battle before, but he certainly earned some respect from God, who approached him as one who was worthy of leadership. God knew that one can be physically strong, but cowardly, or one can be brave of heart despite physical weakness.

God chose Gideon to free the people of Israel and condemn their worship of idols. In the beginning it may have looked like he was immensely unsure of himself and requested that God provide proof of his intentions. After God performed a couple of miracles to show his level of intent, Gideon destroyed the town's altar to Baal and Asherah. He then sent out messengers to gather together men from other tribes who would be willing to stand up and meet an enemy force that had camped on their land.

After they had all gathered together, 32000 strong, God informed Gideon that he had too many men and instructed him to send home those who were afraid. I have always wondered how Gideon knew they were afraid. Did they fill out a questionnaire or did they conduct interviews? I once heard a statement that the movement produced by the faith of another is quite a different thing from personal faith. The faith of 22000 men was not enough to face the enemy before them and they knew it so God gave them a way out, 22,000 men returned home and 10,000 remained.

The Lord still thought Gideon had too many men. He told him to take them down to the water, and He would separate them there. Gideon did as he was asked. Three hundred men scooped up water in their hands and lapped it, all the others got down on their knees to drink. God told Gideon to keep the three hundred and send everyone else home.

Gideon raised an army of 32,000, but after several of these tests, the Lord whittled the force down to 300 men. God did this so the people of Israel would not boast to Him that they saved themselves by their own strength. God knew that a worthy leader always attracts many people but wasn't interested so much in quantity as he was in quality. God led Gideon in a process that would flush out those who would hinder and find those who would help. After losing 99% of his available resources, and waiting until nightfall, Gideon and his "forlorn hope" attacked the Midianite camp. He gave each of his men a trumpet, a torch, and a clay jar. If it were me I would have thought someone in the command structure had lost a marble or two. Attack an entire army with horns, torches and jars? Gideon was asking his men to trust him as he trusted the Lord, which, as history tells us, is exactly what they did. They quietly surrounded the enemy camp, hiding their torches inside the jars. At Gideon's signal, every man blew his trumpet and broke his jar. The Midianites thought they were being attacked by a numerically far superior force and turned on one another in their haste to retreat. The confused survivors beat a hasty path out of Israel. Midian never recovered, and the land was at peace for 40 years during Gideon's lifetime. He returned home, had 70 sons and died an old man. His victory over the Midianites was remembered for many generations as the "Day of Midian" and as with all the Mighty Men of Valor, there are many things we can learn from Gideon. We learn that leaders are not born but rather are made through carefully developed faith, thoughts, and actions. They become who they are meant to be because of their attitudes.

Gideon had a certain selflessness that made him worthy of being called a Mighty Man of Valor by the Angel of the Lord. I don't believe the Angel was referring to Gideon's attributes at the current time but rather was referring to what he knew he might become. If we, as men, are to enter into a mentoring relationship with someone we must always remember that the way they are now will eventually give way to who they might become, given the right guidance. It is up to us to provide that guidance and we will not accomplish much if we don't begin with these foundations in place. George Washington lost most of the battles he fought but won the Revolutionary War. Teddy Roosevelt was sickly and asthmatic as a youngster. He had to sleep propped up in bed or slouching in a chair during much of his early childhood, and had frequent ailments, but he became one of the most famous Presidents the United States ever had. History doesn't evaluate a person based on where they came from, but rather on where they ended up, and neither should we.

Gideon didn't stop to think of how the outcome of the battle might affect him personally. He was called on by God to deliver the people from this enemy, and he never once thought of himself first. He only thought of the people and how it might affect them. God honors this kind of selflessness and Gideon went on to win one of the greatest battles in the Bible by allowing God to work through him.

This same principle is true in our own lives. We, as men, have missed the boat somewhat because we sometimes think it's all about us when it's really about the people we lead and therefore need to serve. When a group of people, whose only interest is themselves, is put first then the group is less likely to achieve its goals (what?). As creatures of habit, we tend to duplicate the same behaviors as the people around us. So when it comes to disciplining ourselves to not be selfish, we typically need someone to show us how it is done. There is a certain type of humility and perspective that Gideon had which teaches us how to become worthy Mighty Men of Valor ourselves. We can learn from Gideon's actions and then model that same behavior in our lives. We sometimes must become less so that others may become more, thereby effecting change in the lives around them.

Mighty Men are willing to sacrifice
For many years the license plates of New Hampshire bore the slogan, made famous by Revolutionary War general John Stark - "live free or die." The irony is that those great words were printed onto the license plates by inmates in the state prison. They could not leave their prison, but many of us stay in our prisons when we have the power to leave. We want to live free, but we do not want to do what the gospel says we need to do to be truly free - J. Michael Shannon, PREACHING, March/April 2004, p. 61.

The Battle of Thermopylae and the last stand of 300 Spartans has gone down in history as a shining example of courage and sacrifice in the face of overwhelming odds but is a prime example of individuals being willing to do whatever is necessary.

Led by the Spartan King Leonidas, the Greeks resisted the incursion of the vast Persian army under the command of Xerxes I of Persia. The Greeks chose the pass at Thermopylae for their stand because of the narrow confines created by the opposing cliffs. The pass was only 300 feet wide and the only road between Thessaly and Greece passed through it, making it the natural choice for halting the Persian advance.

Accounts of the size of Xerxes force are varied, but most modern historians agree that roughly a quarter of a million assorted Persians and their allies faced the Spartans and their friends that day. The Greeks arranged their forces in formations that grouped the volunteers from each city-state fighting into their own units. Each Persian assault was driven back with heavy loss of life. His failure to dislodge the Greeks threw Xerxes into such a terrible rage that he even had some of his commanders executed.

Leonidas had left 1000 volunteers to guard the Greek rear but were surprised by the Persians and with no stomach for the fight, they fled. Despite the hopelessness of his position, Leonidas resolved to continue his defense of the pass. Most of the Greeks left except for 300 Spartans who resolved to make this their last stand. The reason that they chose to stay is lost on most people. It wasn't because of some high and mighty noble idea of honor or because of overcoming impossible odds. It was because they knew if they didn't make a stand here they would eventually have to make one in their own back yards. They did it to give the other Greek states time to mobilize their armies and also to give their families time to prepare. Knowing he had no hope of winning, Leonidas advanced his troops further out into the pass. They fought until their spears were broken, resorting then to their swords, and then to rocks, bare hands, and even teeth. The Persians brought up their archers and rained arrows onto the Greek position. The few survivors were eventually overwhelmed in a final attack. Leonidas and his troops were willing to do whatever was necessary in order to gain their countrymen the time they needed.

I have always wondered why the people who think leaders are born seem to be followers themselves. No true leader believes that they were endowed with some fantastic gift at birth. They know that it is an honor that they must win every day. They know it is the result of a process that everyone who wishes to be a leader must go through. My questions are: Are you willing to do what is necessary to ensure the safety and success of your family? Are you willing to be the example your children need? Gideon didn't want to lead the army against Israel's foes. He wanted to thresh wheat so he could provide his family with bread. Sometimes we are called upon to be in situations not of our choosing and outside of our comfort zones.

A friend of mine recently had his car broken into while parked on a downtown city street in broad daylight. It is hard to imagine that there wasn't someone standing nearby or walking past that didn't see this crime being committed and say to themselves, "this isn't right, I should do something." But no one did. Not a single eyewitness came forward to say or do anything. Have you ever been in a situation where see something being done that was wrong but you chose not to get involved for fear of your own safety or that of your family? What kind of a message do we send to those around us when we choose to do nothing? We are telling them that it is OK to cower in fear. We say to them, don't get involved, it will work itself out and we will not have to be responsible. Don't be this way! Get involved. Be proactive. Don't concern yourself with the circumstances that brought you to the fight or its aftermath. Stand up and make yourself known should you see injustice in the world. Where do you think we would be if the Founding Fathers of this country stood by and did nothing? We would most likely be a vassal of some other country living pretty much as political and economic slaves.

Mighty Men are willing to do whatever is necessary
In 2002, Master Sgt. Tony Pryor was one of 26 United States Special Forces soldiers who were ordered to raid an al-Qaeda compound in the mountains north of Kandahar, Afghanistan. His men were affectionately known as "door-kickers" or "five minute wonders" due to their SWAT team style tactics at being the first to enter a building. At one point in the raid Sgt. Pryor found himself fighting America's war on terror with his bare hands. Pryor's other squad members had gone to clear the rest of the building, so through a course of events he found himself alone in a room with three of the enemy. He knew that if any got past him they could shoot his buddies in the back. It was his responsibility to win so he shot two of them in the first few seconds and then had to fight the third in hand-to-hand combat. He describes himself being "so close he could smell the man's sour breath."

"'Whatever digging, scratching, biting, hair-pulling, ear-ripping-off tactics you have to employ; whatever you got to do to get the job done, that's what you do" Pryor says, explaining the actions that won him the Silver Star for heroism and saved the lives of the other team members in the building. Sgt. Pryor is a living testimony as to how we as Mighty Men should confront every challenge we encounter. No army has ever taken the field expecting to lose, so we as Mighty Men should go in expecting to win.

In Ernest Gordon's true account of life in a World War II Japanese prison camp, "Through the Valley of the Kwai", there is a story that never fails to move me. It is about a man who, after giving up everything he had, literally transformed a whole camp of soldiers. The man's name was Angus McGillivray. Angus was a Scottish prisoner in one of the camps filled with Americans, Australians, and Britons who had helped build the infamous Bridge over the River Kwai. The camp had become an ugly situation where a literal dog-eat-dog mentality had set in. Allies would literally steal from each other and cheat each other; men would sleep on their packs and yet have them stolen from under their heads, survival was everything. The law of the jungle prevailed...until the news of Angus McGillivray's death spread throughout the camp. Rumors spread like wildfire upon his death. No one could believe Angus had given in. He was strong, one of those who they had expected to be the last to die. Actually, it wasn't the fact of his death that shocked the men, but the reason he died. After a fashion, they finally pieced together the true story.

The Argylls (Scottish soldiers) took their buddy system very seriously. Their buddy was called their "mucker," and these Argylls believed that is was literally up to each of them to make sure their "mucker" survived. Angus's mucker, though, was dying, and everyone had given up on him, everyone, of course, but Angus. He had made up his mind that his friend would not die. Someone had stolen his mucker's blanket. So Angus gave him his own, telling his mucker that he had "just come across an extra one." Likewise, every mealtime, Angus would get his rations and take them to his friend, stand over him and force him to eat them, again stating that he was able to get "extra food." Angus was going to do anything and everything to see that his buddy got what he needed to recover.

116

But as Angus's mucker began to recover, Angus collapsed, slumped over, and died. The doctors in the camp discovered that he had died of starvation complicated by exhaustion. He had been giving of his own food and shelter. He had given everything he had — even his very life. The ramifications of his acts of love and unselfishness had a startling impact on the compound. "Greater love has no man than this, that a man lay down his life for his friends" (John 15:12) says. As word circulated of the reason for Angus McGillivray's death, the feel of the camp began to change. Suddenly, men began to focus on their mates, and their friends other than themselves, living beyond survival and embracing selflessness. They began to pool their talents — one was a violin maker, another an orchestra leader, another a cabinet maker, another a professor. Soon the camp had an orchestra full of homemade instruments and a church called the "Church without Walls" that was so powerful, so compelling, that even the Japanese guards attended. In time, the men began a university, a hospital, and a library system. The place was transformed; and in it love was revived, all because one man named Angus gave all he had for his friend. For many of those men this turnaround meant survival. What happened is an awesome illustration of the potential unleashed when one person actually gives it all away. - Holy Sweat, Tim Hansel, 1987, Word Books Publisher, pp. 146-147

Gideon, Leonidas, Master Sergeant Pryor, and Angus McGillivray were not *born* Mighty Men. They came from the womb pale and naked just like you and me. They saw the same things as you and me. They heard and felt the same things as you and me. What made them Mighty Men were the decisions they made or were willing to make. Each was placed in situations they didn't want to be in and given responsibilities they didn't want, but instead of whining or complaining they shouldered the weight and moved forward. They didn't question the circumstances or themselves. They were willing and capable of doing whatever was necessary so that someone else would not have to.

Chapter 11
Mighty Men Live By a Code *[No Retreats, No Reserves, No Regrets]*

It is better to sleep on what you plan to do than to be kept awake by what you've done. - Anon

In 1904 William Borden, heir to the Borden Dairy Estate, graduated from a Chicago high school a millionaire. His parents gave him a trip around the world. Traveling through Asia, the Middle East, and Europe gave Borden a burden for the world's hurting people. Writing home, he said, "I'm going to give my life to prepare for the mission field." When he made this decision, he wrote in the back of his Bible two words: No Reserves. Turning down high paying job offers after graduation from Yale University, he entered two more words in his Bible: No Retreats. Completing studies at Princeton Seminary, Borden sailed for China to work with Muslims, stopping first at Egypt for some preparation. While there he was stricken with cerebral meningitis and died within a month. A waste, you say! Not in God's plan. In his Bible underneath the words No Reserves and No Retreats, he had written the words No Regrets. - Our Daily Bread, December 31, 1988

When Julius Caesar led his legions across the Rubicon his actions led to one of ancient history's most pivotal events. Possessing an unmatched political ambition and unsurpassed military skills, Julius Caesar was elected to the highest position in Rome, Consul, in 59 BC. After his required year of service he was named governor of Gaul where he amassed an immense personal fortune and exhibited his outstanding military skill in subduing the native Celtic and Germanic tribes.

Caesar's popularity with the people soared, making the Senate and Pompey, who held power in Rome, somewhat edgy. Accordingly, the Senate called upon Caesar to resign his command and disband his army or risk being declared an "Enemy of the State." Pompey was given the responsibility of enforcing this edict and the foundation for civil war was laid.

Caesar was staying in the northern Italian city of Ravenna and he had a decision to make. Either he did what the Senate asked, or he moved to confront Pompey and plunge the Roman Republic into a bloody civil war. An ancient Roman law, designed to protect the republic from an internal military threat, declared it treasonous for any general to cross the Rubicon and enter Rome with a standing army. What he did at this tiny stream would reveal his intentions and also would be his literal point of no return.

When the news came to Ravenna that his requests in the Senate had been utterly rejected, and that his friends themselves had fled Rome, he stood at the riverbank considering the importance of the step he was about to take. He turned to those about him, saying, "Still we can retreat! But once let us pass this little bridge, - and nothing is left but to fight it out with arms!" Even as he hesitated, a man appeared and played upon a pipe. Some shepherds and soldiers heard him and came flocking from their posts. He snatched a trumpet from one of them and ran to the river with it sounding the "Advance!" with a piercing blast as he crossed the river. At this Caesar cried out, "Let us go where the omens of the Gods and the crimes of our enemies summon us! THE DIE IS NOW CAST!"

Military strategists have studied Caesar's tactics for thousands of years. Might Men can learn much from Julius Caesar and should acquaint ourselves with this fascinating military figure because his thoughts and actions are applicable to us today.

Mighty Men Have No Regrets
Reviewing Caesar's actions before that morning, one can conclude that he had many doubts as to which course of action he must take. On one hand, if he capitulated and surrendered to Pompey, he would have been thrown in jail and possibly even executed. On the other, if he led his legions across the Rubicon he would be branded a traitor, with the same end result. With the same consequences present for either option, Ceaser saw little point in second-guessing himself no matter which he chose.

The bottom line is, if you are alive you will have some regrets. You cannot avoid regret entirely, but you can lessen it somewhat, and you can reduce the severity by making wise decisions. A Mighty Man of Valor should always be ready to inspire others by encouraging them in times of difficulty or challenge. He should always make a point of reminding people why they are working and striving; he should constantly express confidence in them and their ability to overcome whatever challenges they may face. A Mighty Man should never regret using kind words to empower people. Sometimes, you may attempt to encourage someone who is struggling only to find that they prefer to retaliate with harsh words or actions. When that happens don't ask yourself, "why did I waste the time and effort?" We all have regrets and if we allow them to they will bury us in self-pity and recrimination. Regret comes in many forms. Sometime we wish we were more assertive, or had more self-discipline or took more risks. We regret not spending more quality time with our families because the responsibilities at work just keep piling up. The point is that we should never let the regrets become the focus, but rather we should see them for what they really are, stepping stones on our path to accomplishment.

Once, I read a story about a man who never opened the car door for his wife nor did any of the niceties that wives appreciate. He felt such a show of chivalry was silly. "Besides, she doesn't have two broken arms" he would say. This went on for many years until finally the wife died. At the funeral the family waited at the hearse for the pallbearers. When they came, the mortician asked the husband "open the door for her will you?" The man reached for the door handle and suddenly froze. Regret came crashing in on him. He realized he had never opened the car door for her in life; now, in her death, it would be the first, last, and only time.

Mighty Men should always strive to put as much as we can into what is most important in our lives and let God take care of what comes out. Never regret investing in people even though the rewards may not be apparent. Never regret asking people to do something that may be outside their comforts zones. When they succeed they will give you their heart because you challenged them to do better. When they fail they will see the lesson for what it is and learn from it. You will accomplish more when people lend their hearts to the cause than you ever will if they only give you their hands so you should never regret the outcome if you know you did your best.

Though the easy thing to do would have been to surrender and take his chances with the courts and the Senate, Caesar knew he would forever regret that decision. He would always ask himself: What if I had chosen the other path? What would have been the outcome? In his mind it was better to keep pressing forward even though the outcome looked bleak because it would be better to have tried and failed than to have not tried at all.

Mighty Men Hold Nothing Back [No Reserves]
Mighty Men should always be prepared to give everything. Caesar did! He was completely and utterly committed to his men and their mission because to be otherwise meant certain death for them all. If we as men did everything we needed to do with that same sense of urgency can you imagine what we might accomplish? I am not saying that we need to treat every situation as a life or death ordeal but if we applied that same mindset to something as simple as paying attention to your spouse when she is speaking, I think we would be surprised at what can be accomplished. Listen with your ears and your mind. It may also be as drastic as giving your life in defense of your nation, something every one of us should be ready to do because to lose our freedom means losing our ability to provide hope to someone who has none. Would you rather die for something you know is right, or live, only to be known as a coward? We all want to be the hero in every situation but we are held back by fear. Fear of what people might think. Fear of what they might do. Fear of being fearful. We fear failure to the point that we do not act, then we loath ourselves because of our inaction. A hero is not someone who has a lack of fear; a hero is someone who will step in and do what's right despite the fear within them, holding nothing back. So again...we must ask ourselves, what holds us back? Do we fear the loss of control in the situation or do we fear actually having control of the situation and then being held responsible for the outcome?

General Charles Gordon served the British military for many years in China. When the English government wished to reward him for his service, he declined all monetary offers, but accepted a gold medal inscribed with his name and a record of his battles. At his death the medal was found missing. Later it was learned that during a famine in Manchester, he donated it to be melted and sold to buy bread for the poor.

121

In his diary that day he wrote, "the last and only thing that I had in this world that I valued, I have given over to the Lord Jesus Christ."

Are you willing to give everything you have to keep your marriage together? This will require training. Will you stand up, swallow your pride and arrogance and become the Mighty Man of Valor that your family so desperately needs? This will take a certain amount of equipping. It may not have even been your fault but does it really matter in the end? Ask yourself, is the lifelong promise you both made more important than the outcome of one single act? You will have to care enough to make something happen. The Mighty Man of Valor should always be ready to train, equip, and care for those he have been given leadership over. In as much as those attributes are necessary in your own life, they will be even more important to the people in your trust. If you don't show leadership in passing along these attributes, the people in your care will never live up to the potential within them.

Mighty Men Do Not Retreat
Caesar felt that a great leader had to establish himself as the prime example to his men and to do this he had to be the ideal model for them, especially enduring hardship. He never retreated from any challenge. Caesar's march to Rome was a work in progress. Not knowing that Caesar had only one legion with him and fearing the worst, the Senate offered Pompey their backing, which he neither denied nor accepted. Realizing that Rome was in danger, he made the statement, "Rome cannot be defended" and with the reigning consuls, and the more conservative senators, fled the city. This retreat was later reflected on by Cicero to be an "outward sign of weakness," giving Caesar time to consolidate his forces in his quest for eventual dictatorship.

During the Battle of Thermopylae, Daxos the Arcadian tried to convince King Leonidas of Sparta to either retreat or surrender as his allies had deserted him and his 300 Spartans held the pass against a numerically overwhelming force of Persians alone.

Daxos: Glory? Have you gone mad? There is no glory to be had now! Only retreat, or surrender or death!

King Leonidas: Well, that's an easy choice for us, Arcadian! Spartans never retreat! Spartans never surrender! Go spread the word. Let every Greek assembled know the truth of this. Let each among them search his own soul. And while you're at it, search your own.

We as Mighty Men would do ourselves well to adopt the mindset of the ancient Spartans. We all are faced with challenges that seem to bombard us from every direction. When you find out your teenager may be doing drugs, don't ignore it and tell yourself it's just a phase they are going through. Search your own soul and then confront them! If you find out your best friend is having an affair, don't sit back and tell yourself it's none of your concern. Challenge them! If you see a man and woman having a physical confrontation, don't stand there and say, it's none of my concern. Get involved! If you discover that you made a mistake at work, don't try to push it under the rug or blame someone else. Stand up and take the heat! Sometimes, our first inclination is to run or to hide hoping the challenge will either go away or pass us by. Instead, we need to turn and face the problem. We as Mighty Men must form the habit of dealing with it when it's right in front of us. We must never retreat from that which we know we must face because to do otherwise only makes the problem worse. Giving up gives our opponents the satisfaction of admitting that they were right. Eleanor Roosevelt once said,

"You gain strength, courage, and confidence by every experience in which you really stop to look fear in the face. You are able to say to yourself, "I have lived through this horror. I can take the next thing that comes along.'

The motivation to tell yourself that you will not retreat has to come from within and needs to be of such strength that when the pangs of self-doubt, fear and insecurity approach, you know they may be overcome. You will have to push forward and believe in your heart that you will succeed because you know there is no looking back. Mighty Men of Valor never retreat nor do they do anything with any less than everything they have. They also do everything so as to never have regrets stem from their actions (or inactions).

Chapter 12
Mighty Men of Valor are Men of Faith

"Looking ahead. Giving direction. Anticipating needs. Defining the destination. What makes a man? First, foremost, and above all else, it is vision. A vision for something larger than himself. As men we often misplace our vision. We focus myopically on houses and cars and stock portfolios and bank accounts and piling up stuff. We imagine status and security in these things, when in fact there is no status or security if you don't have relationships. Too many guys squander their vision—and then wonder why they lose their families. It's the all too common downside to superficial definitions of success, and don't let anyone snow you, nothing makes up for the failure of a family" (Tender Warrior, Stu Weber, pp. 24, 25).

In 2007, Lisa and I decided to sell our house. We decided to do this even though the real estate market at the time was in the tank. We even went so far as to price the house somewhat higher than most other properties around us. Honestly, we did this because we needed the money. We had purchased the house two years earlier, completely remodeled it, and then decided to sell it and move closer to Lisa's parents. Our agent thought we were crazy. Some of our "friends" went so far as to offer their unqualified advice as to what we should and shouldn't do but we knew that if God wanted it to happen then nothing would stop Him.

Four months went by. We had tons of people looking at our house but no one made an offer. In the meantime the market kept getting worse and we began to wonder if we had made the right decision. We even went so far as to begin to second guess whether God had spoken to us in the first place and placed us upon this course of action. But, one day when neither of us had even given it a second thought, God decided to move. A couple came by one Sunday afternoon and just fell in love with our house. They even went so far as to take a second look in the same afternoon. That evening our agent called us and I believe her exact words were "you two have to be the luckiest people alive." Apparently this couple had gone back and wrote a contract offer for our house and not just any offer either. They wrote a full price contract! Our agent kept saying she couldn't believe it.

For someone to do something like that in the market at the time was completely unheard of. I told her that we were not lucky, but rather were blessed. I told her that Lisa and I had a personal, one-on-one, daily conversational relationship with the God in Heaven who controls and owns everything. The way we saw it was that the house was really his and we were just renting it until he decided to move us somewhere else.

There was one small glitch in the whole thing though. When one sells a house, at the request of the buyer's lender, a home appraisal is performed. This is done to make sure that the house is being sold at fair market value. I honestly began to worry some at this point because remember we were in a "down" market and some houses near us had already sold for less than what we were asking, which may have a detrimental effect on the whole sale. I knew I could look up the sales numbers myself, but after a few days of prayer I realized again that this entire process was God's doing and His will would be done no matter what. So I decided not to look at the numbers and take a step out on faith.

So how does the story end? The sale fell through. The appraisal didn't come in high enough due to a number of factors and that meant that the buyers would have had to come up with the difference between the appraisal and the asking price. Some of you are sitting here right now and saying to yourselves, well I guess your faith wasn't strong enough! What you don't realize is that my faith was just fine. It just wasn't Gods plan for us to sell our house. The possibility exists that Lisa and I may have misunderstood what God was telling us to do, but only by taking action would we find out. See, I had faith that if God willed it, He would sell our house. It wasn't due to any lack of faith on my part but rather a lack of will on God's. He knew what was best for us at that particular time and the selling of our house wasn't it. Personally, looking back, I think it God was testing our resolve and faith in his will for our lives.

God is going to test you in certain ways and at certain times to see just how faithful you really are. He wants to know if you are just all talk or does your walk match your talk. He wants to know if you are going to take action based on faith or if you will sit and wait for a better opportunity. All of us need to realize that there comes a point that we cannot do it alone and we are going to have to eventually turn to Him for help and reassurance. In my opinion, having faith is doing this before you are backed against the wall. Faith is not reacting to the circumstances. It is responding to the outcome of the circumstances. Faith without action will fail. Faith is acting on what you believe. "God helps those who help themselves" is not in the Bible but it is a biblical concept. Faith has to be active to be of any value. Remember the fellow who had leprosy and God told him he had to go dip in the river in order to be healed? In faith, he had to believe and do what he could. Like the poor woman who had to collect containers to hold all that oil God was giving her - she did what she could by taking action.

If you have ever seen the movie Indiana Jones and the Last Crusade you will know what stepping out on faith is. Jones and his companions reach the Canyon of the Crescent Moon, the site of the temple housing the Grail. The Nazis capture them in the temple, and Donovan shoots Indiana's father, forcing him to retrieve the Grail, so as to heal his father's fatal wounds. Guided by his father's diary, Indiana has to cross an invisible bridge. He cannot see it but he has to make the decision in his heart that it is there none the less. He has to take a literal step of faith in order to reach a room where a knight of the First Crusade, kept alive by the power of the Grail, has hidden it among many false cups.

Our lives are like that sometimes. We know that we must take the step forward but fear, which is an outward manifestation of lack of faith, holds us back. There will be times when we must ignore the facts and move forward on faith. We will face challenges that make absolutely no sense. There will be no easy answers and in these times we will find out just what kind of Mighty Man of Valor we truly are. We must learn to move even though the tangible evidence screams at us to do otherwise. When you get to the end of the tunnel and you know it's time to step out into the light of the unknown, faith is knowing that one of two things will happen; either you will be given something solid to stand on or you will be taught how to fly.

When Nebuchadnezzar invaded Judah and conquered Jerusalem, a guy by the name of Daniel and three of his friends named Shadrach, Meshach, and Abednego were among the Jewish nobility carried off to Babylon as hostages and advisors. Daniel and his three Jewish companions were marched almost 1000 miles from their home to Babylon where they were subsequently evaluated and chosen for their intellect to be trained as advisors to the Babylonian court.

Babylon was an ancient city in the plain of Shinar on the Euphrates River, about 50 miles south of Modern Baghdad. It was founded by Nimrod in Genesis 10, who developed the world's first organized system of idolatry. It must have been a bit overwhelming to the four Jewish boys, the temptation to succumb to the religious and moral practices of the Babylonians must have been overwhelming to them. However, Daniel and his three companions fought the influences of the world around them and remained fiercely loyal to their Jewish religious and cultural identity, an identity which would later come into conflict with the paganism of the Babylonian court. In short, Daniel's faith would be tested to the extreme.

Daniel's training was designed to prepare him for service to the empire. He distinguished himself during this period for his piety, and for his strict adherence to his own morals. These traits won him the esteem of those who were over him. When Daniel spoke, people listened; he was the E.F. Hutton of his day. While we are here I think there is a lesson to be learned. If we stand up for what we believe and hold true to our convictions there will be some who will chastise and ridicule us for no other reason other than that we are different, but there will be even more who will look at us as shining examples of something that they themselves want to be. People *will* respect you for not changing course on a whim, like a reed in a swirling wind, even though they themselves may not share your beliefs and convictions.

After three years of discipline and training in the royal Babylonian schools, Daniel soon rose to the rank of governor of the province of Babylon, which effectively made him responsible for all state affairs. Think about this for a second. Here is a guy who refuses to give up his ideals and heritage while living amongst the most backsliding, immoral politicians and government officials of a country not his own. He even took a shot at interpreting Nebuchadnezzar's dreams;that, alone, could have gotten him killed if he ever misinterpreted them or for whatever reason they didn't turn out as he said.

Daniel's faith in God exposed him to all kinds of persecution by jealous rivals within the king's administration. As time went on, Daniel's successes resulted in his and his companion's promotion, which made him untouchable. But he and his companions did become vulnerable to accusations that had them thrown into the furnace for refusing to worship the Babylonian king as a god. In most arenas, whether they be corporate or political, no matter how well you do there will always be someone looking to bring you down. This is when you will need your faith the most. You will eventually need to rely on something or someone bigger than yourself or anyone around you. There will come a point when the challenge can only be overcome by a God-sized solution and He will want to know that you believe He can do it.

So the king throws Daniel's three buddies into a blazing hot furnace for nothing more than refusing to worship his statue. He had a memorial to himself constructed 90 feet high and 9 feet wide, to which the entire nation was commanded to bow down. This was not merely an act of respect toward the king, but was intended as an act of worship and idolatry. Daniel's three young friends found this something they neither could nor would do, even on penalty of death. It was tantamount to you refusing to go out drinking with the boss after work on Friday. Yeah, it was that big of a deal!

The king had a spectacular ceremony planned. A huge crowd was assembled, virtually all who lived in Babylon would be gathered for worship, the awesome golden edifice standing tall above the crowds. Not far away, the furnace was burning and everyone knew they must choose between the two. It was the image or the furnace, bow down or burn. Daniel's friends took their leap of faith and told the king "No Way Dude!" [My paraphrase] knowing full well that it would mean their lives. They knew deep down in their Mighty Man souls that God would deliver them and that nothing on this earth could hurt them. Even some really man-sized barbecue!

The three Hebrews, bound and still in their festive dress, were carried to the furnace and then thrown in. The fire was so hot that those charged with the unpleasant task of throwing the men into the fire were consumed by the flames themselves. These three men did not stand a chance but they didn't need one because when one has faith one does not need chances.

130

And they were miraculously and faithfully saved.

The king and his officials now witnessed the full extent of the miracle God had performed for them. Neither their clothing nor their bodies had been harmed by the intense heat and flames. Their hair had not been singed nor was there even the smell of smoke upon them. Their deliverance could not have been more complete. The only thing they lost in those flames were the ropes which bound them.

Their example in the furnace that day set a legal precedent of immense importance in Babylon. It determined the way religion was to be practiced in Babylon for years. You and I may never be called upon to make that kind of sacrifice to reveal the depths of our faith but we may be asked to reveal it other, smaller ways. We need to have faith when our children leave the house everyday for school. We need to know in our hearts that they will be taken care of and kept safe. We need to have faith when our wives are ill and the doctors cannot determine why. Faith has to be our foundation when one of our loved ones volunteers for military service in a war. We need to rely on something much bigger than ourselves so that when the challenges do come, there is a sense of calm in us that tells the world, it's no big deal we can overcome it. Everyone who may one day hope to become a Mighty Man of Valor will one day reach a crossroads of faith when they will have to make a stand, even at the risk of huge personal loss. It is during these times, and yes there will be more than one, when your courage, conviction, and faith will guide you to the solution.

Years later, Daniel was cast into a den of lions for continuing to practice his faith, and was miraculously delivered. Daniel had remained true to his faith and to his God and since he made no attempt to hide this, was caught praying. It was against the law to recognize any other deity except those approved by the state. Some of Daniel's contemporaries were jealous of his success, and turned him in. When the king was told, he was greatly distressed because he liked Daniel and did everything he could to save him. But even he had to obey the law and so at sundown he was forced to give the order to have Daniel arrested. As he watched Daniel being lowered into the lions' den he said to him, "Your God whom you serve continually, He will deliver you." Then he sealed up the den, went home and, refusing to eat, spent a sleepless night alone. Even the king had faith in the eventual outcome. At dawn's first light, the king went to the pit called out to Daniel "Has your God whom you serve continually been able to save you?" Daniel answered. "O King live forever. My God sent His angel and he shut the lions' mouths. They have not hurt me because I was found innocent in His sight. Nor have I done anything wrong before you, O King." The king, to put it mildly, was overjoyed and gave the order to have Daniel removed from the lions' den. There was no wound or scratch on him. The king then had the men who had falsely accused Daniel rounded up and thrown into the lions' den along with their families. Before they reached the floor of the den, the lions were upon them. After which the king issued a decree declaring reverence for "the God of Daniel." Daniel's faith in God probably did more to put an end to the Jewish Captivity than any other event or person.

I often wonder how many of us are willing to stand up for our faith on a daily basis. How many of us have been in an office environment and someone takes the Lord's name in vain? Do we take them aside and explain to them the errors of their ways or are we more in fear of being rejected by them than we are of the Most High God whom we serve? Are we so trapped in our politically correct worlds that we won't even defend God for fear of having those around us chastise us? What happens when we see our own children acting in a way that does not exemplify their biblical teaching and upbringing? Do we try to be their best friend and hope that they will still like us afterwards or do we become the father they so desperately need? Mighty Men never wait to survey the mood of the people in the hope of gaining the most personally beneficial outcome. This is a great way to paralyze your character and your organization. Your convictions must be acted upon and done so decisively.

Faith is developed through character
Daniel was a man of character. He wanted what God wanted. Are we the same way? His life was utterly and completely devoted to God but he still managed to perform the duties given to him by his less than positive superiors. Today, it is easy to get caught up in negative thinking. The easier path always seems to be to expect the worst. We must take action to stop this thought cycle. Your actions must be the outward portrayal of your faith. The results of not doing what is required will be played out in negative emotions that can become emotional problems such as depression

132

and anxiety. If we really want to see change we must constantly monitor our lives and work. If we think changes must be made then we must make them. Sometimes that will mean stepping out on faith. It is really about "putting your money where your mouth is!"

Faithful men have a warrior's spirit

Daniel also had a warrior's spirit within him; and because of this, he rose to positions of high leadership. This is what God wants for us today. He wants Christian men to take their rightful place in their homes, in their community, in their church, and in their nation. He wants us to be in positions where we can be of the most influence. He wants us to live by the same standards that Daniel lived by. Shadrach, Meshach, and Abednego had reached a crossroads in their faith. There had come a point when they must either take a stand or kneel to a false god. They were given one simple choice: bow or die. There was no negotiating or bargaining. There was no "we'll meet you halfway" type of meeting. They chose the furnace. They chose the road less traveled and had the courage to take the first steps. The people were given the opportunity and example to see their gift in action that day. On that day they stood as warriors, not the smooth-faced pampered court liaisons everyone thought they were. They knew as faithful warriors that their God would save them. We as Mighty Men have a day like that coming. There will be a day not too far off when we will be given a choice of whether to stand up for what we believe in or blend into the crowd so that no one will see us. On that day it will be determined whether we are worthy of being men of valor or men of convenience. We will be tried and either found wanting or found to be shining examples of hope.

Faith requires time to grow

Ever heard of the concept of trial and error? Some people are not willing to take action on things of which they are not certain. They don't have the faith necessary to step out on an unsure bet from time to time; they are not willing to take a chance once in a while. What they don't realize is that, over time, faith will produce results, but you have to stay with it. Faith is not a do it once and get it over with type of thing. It is a do it again and again until you get it done type of thing. We sometimes have to stop and remember that anything of value takes time and what can be more valuable than our faith? College takes time. Great jobs take time. Marriage

133

certainly takes time. Raising great kids takes a lot of time. All life takes time and we must first be patient and then faithful to it.

Faith is a matter of choice

As with most things in life, being a man of faith is a choice You choose to wake up and go to work every day. You choose who you want to spend your life with. You choose your friends and they choose you. You choose which church you wish to attend. You choose whether or not to allow the message to direct you. You have chosen, at some point in time, whether or not to believe in God. You may have chosen to believe and commit yourself to a living savior and become born again, but are struggling to overcome your past life with all of its promises and desires. You will choose whether to be a Mighty Man of Valor or a spineless wonder; a member of the vast masses rather than one of the select few. You can be the guy who sticks his head up above the crowd once in a while and takes a few tomatoes in the kisser, or you can be the one who hides and never makes an impact on anyone or anything. In much the same way, you choose to have faith or not. Having faith that the results will manifest themselves requires choice. Having the faith to do the work requires a choice; a choice that will need to be made and which will determine whether you move forward or you retreat. So I challenge you today to, at the very minimum, make a choice. Let go of the meaningless tangible things of this world and step out on the path of faith. Walk in character and integrity and be all that you can be, a Mighty Man of Valor.

Chapter 13
Mighty Men Are Disciplined

No man is fit to command another who cannot command himself.
- William Penn

Picture this. You are standing alone in on the field of battle facing eight hundred mean-looking, snarling, beady-eyed, highly trained and heavily armed soldiers. They are big and burly and look like they know their business. They have a gleam in their eye that can only mean pain for you. They have one purpose and that is to take you down, preferably in little pieces. You know that there is no way you can stand against eight hundred warriors on your own. Your knees feel like yesterdays Jell-O and your palms are as sweaty as today's gym socks. You're facing an immovable mountain, you are unable to go over it or move around it. You know you have to go through it and the only way to do that is to stand and fight. You're facing insurmountable odds, but even in the midst of the terror and apprehension, deep down inside, you can feel the years of discipline steeling your resolve and you know that victory will be yours! Welcome to the life of Adino the Eznite.

I think you should tell the Adino story here since you refer to it throughout the following paragraphs.

From time to time we all feel like we are in this same situation. When God allows a mountain to rise up in our lives we discover we are not able to follow our first instinct and ignore it. We hope and pray that we have the discipline to stand and fight, no matter what the odds may be. We pray we have the inner strength to make a decision and take action until the results have been accomplished, regardless of any inner or outer resistance. We rely on the ability to overcome laziness, temptations, and negative habits no matter what effort may be required.

Adino only had one solution to his problem, and that was to depend on God to do battle for him. The amazing thing is that God is willing to do the same for you if you will only let him. He wants you to have enough discipline that you trust him even when the whole world seems to be crashing down around you. He wants you to know that you will have safe harbor in his spirit but you must win your way to him first.

I once heard a statement about discipline that I have carried with me for years. It went like this; if you don't do it someone else will. If you don't have it someone will give it to you. I never wanted to be either of those people. We, as men, have to start developing discipline in every area of our lives but in order to do that we must first understand what self-discipline is because no matter how gifted you think you are, your gifts will never reach their maximum potential without the application of self-discipline.

There are some interesting points to be learned from Adino which we as Mighty Men can find useful.

He used what he had
Adino didn't have any worldly help. All his friends had fled and weren't coming back anytime soon. They had all found better things to do and more interesting places to be. He didn't have an armored division or a company of battle-hardened Airborne Rangers at his disposal. He didn't have the best armor made or the biggest, strongest shield money could buy. He had no longbow with which he could pick them off from a distance. The point is he didn't wait for them to come to him before he did something. He had a spear, one single stick with a sharp point, and he made plans to use it. He could only kill one person at a time with it and he would have eight hundred chances to practice with it. We as Mighty Men need to stop complaining about lack of resources. We will not always have all the necessary tools we need to accomplish all our missions. Money will most likely be tight the majority of the time. The teachers will always hate you and your parents will always be out to get you. Your wife will never agree with you completely and your kids will just look at you funny much of the time. You are just going to have to do what you can with what you have. We need to move forward because we know if we do not we will lose. None of the ideas we have will ever come to fruition if we do not do something to move forward, otherwise the impact we know we are supposed to be having will never come about.

He didn't quit just because the odds were against his success

Adino knew how many challenges were in front of him, there were exactly eight-hundred of them. He didn't need to spend time dwelling on facts he already knew. He didn't sit and contemplate the cost beforehand. He knew what the result would be if he didn't do something. We are the same way. We know what will happen if we stop being our children's best friend and start becoming their father. We know what will happen if we continue to stand around and watch the company we work for engage in unlawful practices. We know what will happen if we don't stop our friends from performing their immoral acts. We know what will happen if we don't, so let's focus on what will happen if we do. What will happen if we step forward and let people know what we think and how we feel? What would our wives think if we decided one day to start being the man they so desperately need us to be? All of the great successes we have in this life will come with great price tags so why dwell on the cost? Just be willing to pay it and accept the reward you know is on the other side.

He didn't quit until it was over

When Adino started towards the eight hundred bad guys he knew in his mind that this would not come to an end until either they were down or he was. He committed himself to the long haul no matter the outcome. He knew that it would be a wasted effort if he killed 799 of his adversaries only to have the 800th take his head off. He started this fight with the intention of winning, not just surviving, and we as Mighty Men need to take that same view with the challenges in our lives. If you're going to start a new business, resolve yourself to staying with it until it succeeds. Don't bail the first time something bad happens, and don't even give up the second or third time either. We can apply this same thought process to our marriages. Just because things don't look as good as they did on our wedding day is not an excuse to give up. You gave your word to your wife and the Supreme Commander that you would stick it out until death came looking for you. You swore that no matter what person or event came your way in an attempt to lay siege to your marital castle you would defend it with all your heart and soul. Don't be one of those spineless wonders who gives up every time some challenge comes their way; try to figure out what caused the problem and then work together to make it right. And don't ever quit until you achieve your goal or your tour of duty in this realm is over.

I once read that self-discipline is the ability to take action regardless of your emotional state. This is so true. I used to have days I didn't want to get out of bed because mentally and emotionally I didn't think I could face another day at work...but I did it anyway because I had disciplined myself to the promise I made my employer. I promised them I would show up and do a decent day's work. We all have good intentions when it comes to accomplishing things, but it's our discipline that will actually carry us through. Without self-discipline intentions won't manifest themselves, but with sufficient self-discipline, nothing is impossible.

During the British liberation of Palestine in 1917, while driving up from Beersheba, a combined force of British, Australians and New Zealanders were pressing on the rear of the Turkish retreat over arid desert. The attack outdistanced its water-carrying camel train. Water bottles were empty. The sun blazed pitilessly out of a sky where the vultures wheeled expectantly. "Our heads ached," writes Major V. Gilbert, "and our eyes became bloodshot and dim in the blinding glare...Our tongues began to swell...Our lips turned a purplish black and burst." Those who dropped out of the column were never seen again, but the desperate force battled on to Sheria. There were wells at Sheria, and had they been unable to take the place by nightfall, thousands were doomed to die of thirst.

"We fought that day," writes Gilbert, "as men fight for their lives... We entered Sheria station on the heels of the retreating Turks. The first objects which met our view were the great stone cisterns full of cold, clear, drinking water. In the still night air the sound of water running into the tanks could be distinctly heard, maddening in its nearness; yet not a man murmured when orders were given for the battalions to fall in, two deep, facing the cisterns." He then describes the stern priorities: "The wounded first, then company by company. It took four hours before the last man had his drink of water, and in all that time they had been standing twenty feet from a low stone wall on the other side of which were thousands of gallons of water." - From an account of the British liberation of Palestine by Major V. Gilbert in The Last Crusade, quoted in Christ's Call To Discipleship, J. M. Boice, Moody, 1986, p. 143.

Can you imagine the discipline one had to have to stand so close to the soothing, life-giving water and not run willy-nilly into it? Self-discipline is not a panacea. It will produce results but it will take time. It took time for the British officers to instill this kind of discipline into the troops and it will take time for you to obtain it as well. The challenges which self-discipline can overcome are many. Self-discipline can help you overcome any addiction or accomplish any task. It will destroy procrastination, and disorder. Self-discipline is like a muscle. The more you train it, the stronger you become. The less you train it, the weaker you become.

It took discipline for Benaiah to face the Egyptian and the lion in the pit. Joshua had loads of discipline when day after day he and the Israelites marched around Jericho. Uriah had discipline when he refused to go home and spend time with his family even after his king ordered him to. Shammah the son of Agee had it. He was one of David's top three advisors and was known for standing alone in a field of beans, against Philistines who wanted to rob the people. As a troop of Philistines gathered, the Israelite farmers fled. Shammah, took up a position in the middle of the field and defeated the Philistines. We don't know any of the details other than that, but we know he had to have discipline in his life because when everyone else ran he was still standing. All of these Mighty Men had it and so do you, but just like it was with them, you must learn to develop it one piece at a time and day by day in a systematic way. Learning where to develop it will guide you along the path of learning how to develop discipline in your life. There are many areas in which one can develop discipline, but let's start with the most obvious.

Spiritual
Spiritual discipline begins with your personal commitment. This is an act of the will and a personal decision. After you take that first step, growth can begin but it will take continual investment on your part to increase and strengthen that commitment. There are many actions one can take to become more disciplined in your spiritual life. I personally prefer spending time in devotions. Setting aside time to develop yourself spiritually will benefit you in ways you cannot even begin to imagine when you first start. I begin my day by sitting down with a cup of coffee and my electronic Bible. I like the electronic version because it selects a new passage randomly for me to study every day and then if I have a specific subject I would like to focus on all I have to do is look it up. I read and study then take time to reflect on how the principles I have just

read about can be applied to my own life. It's honestly how the idea for this book got started. I then spend some serious time in prayer asking God for direction and guidance. I thank him for the blessing he has bestowed upon me and also for the challenges he has presented me with. After I am done I take time to read a few pages from a book that will hopefully challenge me to improve in some area of my life. I prefer leadership books but they could be on almost any subject just as long as you're getting something from it that helps you move forward.

I know some of you are sitting there saying "I don't have time for all this!" Part of the challenge of developing discipline in an area of your life is developing the discipline to develop the discipline. It sounds confusing, but look at it this way: If you want to change a habit you have to make the commitment to take the time to change that habit. The same applies with any aspect of your life you wish to change, you have to discipline yourself to devote the time. Maybe it means getting up 30 minutes earlier or going to bed 30 minutes later. It will be hard for the first few days but after that you will find yourself almost craving the time, and if for some reason you miss a day or two you will find yourself working harder to correct it.

Physical
Your wife will not tell you this to your face but you're probably fat. Now before you fly off the handle I am just relaying what I read once and it really opened my eyes to my own physical condition. I had to come to the conclusion in my own mind that I needed to lose weight. I didn't want to admit it but in the back of my mind I knew it was true. A few days later a friend of mine told me something that really jump started me into doing something about it. He said that it's not what you weigh it's what you look like that matters most. I wasn't really concerned with my weight. What bothered me was that my clothes didn't fit and I couldn't stand that I couldn't climb a flight of stairs without wheezing like a freight train. So I disciplined myself to start by doing just a little something everyday. I started doing push ups every morning for 10 minutes. There was no immediate result and I knew there wouldn't be. What changed, though, was that I felt better about myself. I knew I was doing something. Since then I have transitioned into a discipline of running 3 days a week and now I am happy to say I pretty happy with the way I look.

141

One big mistake I see people making when it comes to their physical appearance is the tendency to compare themselves to other people. I know you're doing it because I used to do it and you're just like me. My only advice is this: There will always be someone out there in better shape than you. Don't compare yourself to other people. It won't help. You'll see exactly what you want to see. If you see you're weak, they will seem stronger. If you think you're strong, everyone else will seem weaker. There's no point in doing this. Simply look at where you are now, and aim to get better.

Financial

We all live in what has affectionately been called a "microwave society." That means that we have become a civilization devoted to instant gratification. We mentally tell ourselves, "I want it now" or "I need it now." Financial discipline is what each of us wishes we had but from time to time escapes us due to the fact that we lack discipline. We all wish that we could make our money go farther. We think we should get more out of the money we have. The reason we cannot do everything we want with our money is because we don't do everything we can to produce the money. The reason we do not have that extra cash is because we do not practice financial discipline. It's been said that the definition of insanity is doing the same thing over and over again but expecting different results. If you're not happy with your current financial situation then change it. Don't go out and placate yourself like some bratty child and buy yourself something you cannot afford in an effort to make yourself feel better about not having the money in the first place. Produce a solution, not another problem! Stop and ask yourself *why* you need to purchase that big screen TV. Consider the result of your action three months from now should you decide to buy that bigger house. We have all heard of the game called "Keeping up with the Joneses" and we have all played it at some point. My question was always who were the Joneses and why do I care? Why am I so concerned that their car is brand new and mine is few years old? Is it because my car is causing me problems or is it because I want bragging rights? Did I hit nerve there? Good! Sure, all your friends might drive sports cars and frequently display Swiss watches, but that isn't an excuse for you to do the same. The truth is, many people who have this stuff can't afford it either. By sticking to your budget now, and investing your money properly, you'll find yourself with more money to spend in the long run. A little restraint now will go a long way later. Just remember, it is better to own something lock stock and barrel than it is to own a payment book.

Family

Quality time with the family is not you and the TV. It's you and the members of your family engaged in an activity that allows each of you to determine how the other thinks and reacts. It is getting to know each other on an emotional level. It may be a night playing board games or a day at the beach or it may just be sitting down and having dinner together. When was the last time you asked your wife how her day went? Take time to find out what your kids are thinking about and why. Look for ways of putting them into situations where their thought process becomes evident. Don't let the world outside constantly drag you away from time with your family. Discipline your time with them. Set aside a time each week where the family does something together and don't let anything intrude upon it. Unplug the phone. Turn off the TV (and the Game Boy). Consistently allowing other people and events to distract you from time with your family will seriously erode the credibility you are trying to achieve with your spouse and children.

Career

It takes self-discipline to do a good job or make the most out of your career. Getting ahead takes discipline, which is what enables you to outperform your competition. Discipline will allow your boss, clients, and prospective employers to be impressed because you will develop a professional demeanor through self-control. Work is important and the nice thing about hard work is that anyone can do it. It doesn't matter what industry you're in, hard work can be used to achieve positive long-term results regardless of the specifics involved. When you discipline yourself to do what is hard, you gain access to a realm of results that are denied those who choose not to. Learn to manage your time. Time is non-replaceable, so make the best use of every second. You can show your boss what you really value by the way you spend your time. Interruptions will always happen, so plan for them in your day. "I don't have time" is a sorry excuse and tells the other person that you you see this issue as a lower priority. The time you allow for something will be in direct proportion to your expectations. If it's an urgent problem, it will be done fast. If it's not, it will be done slowly. Discipline yourself to determe where you spend your time.

The Tongue
One of the hardest habits I see people in need of changing is their lack of control when it comes to their tongues. Just because you have an opinion on something doesn't mean that everyone wants to hear it, and disciplining yourself to hold it will save you a lot of grief later on. Learn to talk less and listen more. Listening is not hard to learn but it does require some discipline. Talking less and listening more actually relieves us of the pressure to think of what to say. We'd get in less trouble by not saying the wrong things, or by not saying the right things at the wrong time, or in the wrong way. We also set ourselves apart as being more respectful and caring.

So how do we go about developing discipline in these areas of our lives?

Start small
It's a mistake to try to push yourself too hard when trying to build self-discipline. If you try to reform your entire life overnight, by setting dozens of new goals for yourself and expecting to follow through consistently, you will fail every time. This is like the guy who goes to the gym to start his new workout and without any guidance or self-control packs 300 pounds on the bench press. He either tires quickly or ends up hurting himself.

One of the most effective ways of developing self-discipline is by refusing to satisfy unimportant and unnecessary desires. All of us are constantly presented with an endless stream of temptations, many of which are not really important or productive. By refusing to satisfy them, you become stronger and better at resisting. Rejecting useless desires and actions, and behaving contrary to your habits, strengthens you. The reason temptation is so seductive is that we get sidetracked by what we stand to gain right now, instead of what we stand to gain later. We sacrifice the long term dream for a moment of instant gratification. Let's say you prefer a healthy, strong body six months from now and are working diligently towards that goal. It becomes hard to remain focused when you're staring at a donut dripping with sweet, gooey icing. All you can think about is the pleasure you'll gain from eating the donut now, rather than the benefits you'll gain from sticking to your workout. In order to keep temptation from ruining your efforts at self-discipline, keep a picture of your ultimate goal with you at all times. This may be a photograph from a magazine or a written description of your dream. Tape it to the refrigerator, your steering wheel or the bathroom scale. By keeping the goal in front of you and through constant practice, just like exercising your muscles at a gym, you will increase your ability to harden your resolve.

Here are a few suggestions:

- Turn off the TV and do not turn it on for three days.
- Watch only movies that are rated PG or better for a month.
- Don't read the newspaper for a week or two.
- Listen to an educational CD on your way to work instead of talk radio.
- Refuse to engage in any kind of gossip for a week.
- Read a book for 15 minutes before you go to bed.
- Walk up and down the stairs instead of taking the elevator.
- For a week go to sleep one hour earlier than usual or wake up an hour earlier.
- Drink a bottle of water instead of your usual morning cup of coffee.

These are only a few examples of the many habits one can develop. Much like exercising, we must form a systematic method of training in order to reach our goals, have more control over ourselves or improve some area of our life. Here are a few ideas that might help.

Do the hard work first
A definition of hard work may be the tasks before you that challenge you the most. Most people will take the path of least resistance and do what's easiest. That's exactly why you should do the opposite. You will never get ahead by taking the road most traveled. The shallow opportunities of life will be attacked by hordes of people looking for the easy route. Look at how popular the lottery is in most places. The much tougher opportunities will usually see less competition and result in bigger rewards. When you

145

discipline yourself to take the harder path, you gain access to results that are denied everyone else. List your daily activities in such a way that the most important get done first. This will help you learn to prioritize what needs to be done.

Organize

Self-discipline is formed one decision at a time! Developing self-discipline is an ongoing process, not a one-time event. If you don't already have one, get yourself a calendar and start tracking your habits. Write down your activities each day and then after a week look at where you spend the majority of your time. Use the calendar to keep track of your appointments. You will be amazed at how much more efficient you become at keeping appointments when they are written down in front of you. Check your email every day, maybe even twice a day. Even the small habit you form by doing this will help form a certain level of discipline.

Accept Responsibility

A Mighty Man of Valor knows he can give up almost anything except final responsibility. It's not all going to be a bed of roses. There will be times when you will stumble and fall. Attempting to develop a new habit and not achieving a constant adherence to said habit will help build strength and character. Admitting failure is a much better course of action than trying to cover it up, but also realize that you are never a failure at anything until you quit trying. When people see you off your pedestal and down at their level, trying to overcome the same challenges will establish you as a sincere and credible leader. You will also find that you are able to lead a more productive life if you know what areas you have discipline in and also where you might be lacking. No leader ends up out of bounds without passing the warning signs first.

Developing good discipline can lead to the formation of good habits and habits are mostly the result of tiny daily choices that accumulate. Look at it this way, each choice is a small wire that when woven together with other small wires (choices) eventually form a strong cable (habit). Like a plant that grows a tiny amount each day, our choices accumulate without much notice. By the time we realize we have a habit, the habit has us. Most of our daily choices are made automatically without even thinking about them. To change our habits, we first need to be aware of them and then we need to work backward from the habit to discover what daily disciplines formed it. To change the habit, we need to change those disciplines.

Chapter 14
Mighty Men Are Persistent

Nothing in the world can take the place of persistence. Talent will not; nothing is more common than unsuccessful men with talent. Genius will not; unrewarded genius is almost a proverb. Education will not; the world is full of educated derelicts. Persistence and determination alone are omnipotent. The slogan "Press On" has solved and always will solve the problems of the human race.
- Calvin Coolidge

In 1972, NASA launched the exploratory space probe Pioneer 10. According to Leon Jaroff in Time, the satellite's primary mission was to reach Jupiter, photograph the planet and its moons, and beam data to earth about Jupiter's magnetic field, radiation belts, and atmosphere. Scientists regarded this as a bold plan, for at that time no earth satellite had ever gone beyond Mars, and they feared the asteroid belt would destroy the satellite before it could reach its target. But Pioneer 10 accomplished its mission and much, much more. Swinging past the giant planet in November 1973, Jupiter's immense gravity hurled Pioneer 10 at a higher rate of speed toward the edge of the solar system. At one billion miles from the sun, Pioneer 10 passed Saturn. At some two billion miles, it hurtled past Uranus; Neptune at nearly three billion miles; Pluto at almost four billion miles. By 1997, twenty-five years after its launch, Pioneer 10 was more than six billion miles from the sun. And despite that immense distance, Pioneer 10 continued to beam back radio signals to scientists on Earth. 'Perhaps most remarkable,' writes Jaroff, 'those signals emanate from an 8-watt transmitter, which radiates about as much power as a bedroom night light, and takes more than nine hours to reach Earth.' The Little Satellite That Could was not qualified to do what it did. Engineers designed Pioneer 10 with a useful life of just three years. But it kept going and going. By simple longevity, its tiny 8-watt transmitter radio accomplished more than anyone thought possible. - Craig Brian Larson, Pastoral Grit: the Strength to Stand and to Stay, Bethany.

Perseverance is the dogged determination that allows us to overcome the difficulties in our lives which at times seem at times insurmountable. It was perseverance that enabled Hannibal to cross the Alps in 15 days, the same act took Julius Caesar 11 days, and Napoleon had to have a bit of perseverance to do the same thing in five. Whatever successful effort you choose to undertake in this life will not be accomplished without perseverance. Every Mighty Man of Valor must be able to draw from his personal wellspring of perseverance in order to conquer the challenges before him. Perseverance is the power to accomplish a work without allowing ourselves to be turned aside from the purpose by difficulty or obstacles. It is the art of marching forward while ignoring the inevitable temporary setbacks. People who possess perseverance keep progressing steadily on their chosen path, obstacles seem to strengthen their courage rather than lessen it. The excitement of a challenge seems to sharpen their wits.

Jeremiah the Prophet was one of the most persistent people in the Bible; he just wouldn't quit, give up or back down! There is no question he had one of the toughest assignments of any leader in the Old Testament as he was called to lead a bunch of stiff-necked rebels who would not follow him anywhere. He was born at a time near the end of King Josiah's reign, the last descent (do you mean the last decent king, or the last descendant of the king?)king of Judah. He filled a role when moral standards, political ethics, and religious conventions were on the decline. God asked Jeremiah to deliver a hard message to his people in an effort to raise the standard that had been dropped and recapture their values. Jeremiah saw that Judah was destroying itself through its wicked ways. Although temple worship was still commonplace, the people had corrupted their beliefs with idolatry, stealing, murder, sexual immorality, adultery, and numerous other nasty practices. God decided His people needed to be disciplined. False prophets and corrupt priests told the people that there was no reason to fear Babylon, which at the time was attempting an invasion. Judah had been so taken in by the false prophets that when Jeremiah came along and told them the truth, they violently lashed out at him, persecuting him severely. However, Jeremiah stayed the course set before him. He knew the truth behind God's promises and this caused him to persevere though the most difficult persecution. He faced severe opposition to his preaching from a mob of people and the false prophets but the worse it got the stronger Jeremiah seemed to become.

149

God sent Jeremiah to preach at the temple, to tell all the people of the coming calamity headed for Jerusalem. The chief priest heard Jeremiah's prophecies and had him beaten and put in stocks overnight in an effort to quiet him. But Jeremiah, being mighty in faith, spoke out! He continued to preach, warning the people of their impending doom if they didn't stop treating God like a plot of land and a building standing on it. They thought that living near the temple would protect them from any enemy and they kept ignoring him, but Jeremiah kept right on talking. Instead of accepting truth, they grabbed him and threatened to kill him. At this point many in the same situation would back down, but not Jeremiah. Instead of giving up, he spoke up even more confidently and charged them again. When it seemed as though Jeremiah's adversaries had the best of him he stood up even stronger and more powerfully than before. Jeremiah's perservered in his preaching, resulting in many of the mob changing their minds and saving his own life.

Jeremiah was like the guy that the board of directors hires to replace a CEO for a company ready to go under. His job is to turn things around and overhaul the whole operation. His challenge lay in the fact that he didn't have a single company to work with, he had an entire country on the brink of spiritual bankruptcy and the only thing between them and destruction was how persistent he was with his message. He hung on tight to his task through years of rejection and punishment and he continued to dedicate himself in the furtherance of the cause even though some considered him a traitor. Jeremiah knew that the rejection wasn't fatal, it was merely someone's opinion.

Never at any period in our history is a sense of persistence more necessary in you as a man. The battle for moral reform, political conversion, and religious renewal has become more bitter and protracted for those engaged in it. The number of people who wander blindly through life willing to give up when the times get tough increases every day but victory can be ours if only we are willing to keep "our hands to the plow" and persevere just a bit longer. We must set the example that others may follow. If we recognize the enemies such as laziness, discouragement, lack of confidence, and impatience that constitute the attack on our perseverance, we are much more able to protect ourselves. We learn that there are actions we can consciously take to solidify our ability to persevere in times of strife.

You show perseverance when you:

- Give up your TV time to do more productive things
- Take up a new sport that is very difficult and not quit.
- Have missed a day of work but you work hard to catch up
- You are at the end of a difficult race but you cross the finish line instead of quitting
- Save money and make sacrifices to buy something
- Spend hours practicing a particular hobby
- Study and work hard to finish school
- Try something you weren't successful at the first time

Here are a few simple rules you can follow in your quest to become more perseverant.

Don't give up too early
During the California gold rush, a prospector named R.U. Darby helped his uncle mine a vein of gold that he had discovered. It appeared at first that they had a prosperous find. Yet the vein soon disappeared, and Darby and his uncle searched frantically for the spot where it continued. Finally, they concluded their prospects were hopeless and sold their equipment to a junk dealer. The junk dealer, on a whim, consulted an engineer, and then began mining the shaft again. He quickly discovered the elusive vein and a supply of gold worth millions of dollars, just three feet from where Darby and his uncle had stopped digging. The story brings to light how the worthwhile battles in life are often won by simple persistence. It reminds us that we can give up on a goal too easily and are sometimes much closer to achieving success than we realize.

When something begins to challenge you, wait as long as you can before you express any frustration. If it still doesn't work right, try again and don't lose your temper when it doesn't work that time either. This is what persistence is. It's always finishing what you start no matter the eventual outcome. It's working on a difficult project until you complete it; it's working a little harder or a few minutes longer on a task that you do not

151

like. It's getting up one more time after you have been knocked down. Persistence is taking one more hit and knowing that if you can take enough the other guy will eventually wear out.

When I was younger, and a member of the Boy Scouts of America, I was on the fast track to receive my Eagle rank. I had done everything right and had done it at the appointed time. I had worked harder than anyone else and passed my review boards easily. When it came time to go before the board to review my service for consideration of advancement to the Life Rank, I ran into a bit of a snag. The Life Rank is the last step before Eagle and can be the toughest challenge to anyone seeking to go the distance. As one continues to develop their leadership skills, the Life Scout rank is earned by fulfilling additional leadership positions, service hours, and merit badges. A Life Scout is expected to be a role model and leader in the troop, providing guidance to new scouts and helping out however he can. I had done all the mechanics but found I was missing a key ingredient. The way I found out was through a hard lesson taught to me by someone who would eventually become a mentor of mine.

Charles Olson was the father of one of my great friends, David, and he was also the assistant scoutmaster at the time. It was his responsibility to sit on each review board and examine the candidate's record to make sure they met the qualifications. The night I stood before him he asked me one simple question which I still remember today. He asked "why do you want to be a Life Scout?" I honestly was stumped. I had performed all the tasks and achieved the required number of merit badges. I thought the reason for becoming a Life Scout was because it was the next step towards the ultimate goal. That wasn't the right answer. In a totally unemotional voice he informed me that I had failed and that I would not be able to retake the examination until I was confident I could answer that one question. I was mad! I was thunderstruck! And in a small place in my mind I was ready to pack it in, a voice suddenly spoke up and began to whisper to me, "Why go on? You'll never get by him anyway" after a couple of days fuming and generally making life miserable for everyone within throwing distance, my Dad finally brought me back to reality by asking yet another simple question, "What are you going to do give up?"

My Dad knew which button to push. There is one thing I hate more than anything else in this world and that is someone, anyone, questioning my ability to meet a challenge. He knew I wanted to be an Eagle and the only real question was whether or not I was willing to persist in going after it. Three weeks later I stood before the board and again was asked the same question by Mr. Olson, "The reason one chooses to attempt attainment of the Life Rank is so that he may show the others that he leads that it is possible and that they themselves can do it to. It is not recognition of my hard work but really a picture of how many people I have been given the privilege of helping along the way." Mr. Olson stood up, shook my hand, and informed me that my service and perseverance had paid off. I could now consider myself a Life Scout.

Don't Wait for Things to Change
The grass will never get cut. The car will never get fixed. The dream job will never come along. The roof will never stop leaking and the kids will never become more obedient if we sit around wait for these things to happen. Perseverance and failure cannot exist in the same space. Persevere enough and failure eventually gets shoved out of the way. Failure happens when you quit. When all is said and done, nothing can replace perseverance. From learning to walk to driving a car, life teaches us that failure only occurs when we stop trying. It's a lesson many of us need to take to heart. Then we need to consciously take steps that keep us moving forward. For example, the world is full of those who "tried" to get a business going. After meeting with difficulty or rejections, they quit. They accepted failure, and faded back into the crowd never to be heard from again. The worst part is not that they quit their business and their friends but that they quit themselves. Succeeding at any endeavor may require us to stumble at first. It's part of the learning process. Ultimately, when we persevere through the challenges we learn enough to walk and then run. Remember the words of Vince Lombardi, "We never lost a game, we just ran out of time."

Keep your goal in sight
I cannot remember where I first heard this story but it illustrates in fine fashion how important it is to keep our goals in front of us.

Robert Smith was seated in the lounge at the airport in Sydney, waiting to take the midnight flight to Los Angeles. He had reached the airport hours before schedule and was already tired of sitting idly. Oh, how many times he had mentally rehearsed his speech for the all-important meeting in LA! Tired of idling around, he decided to take a stroll - after all, he had checked in his baggage and there was still almost an hour left before he would be let inside the gate. He decided to go out for a stroll. After the crowd and the noise inside the airport, the cool air outside and the quiet of the night were a welcome change for Robert. He decided to venture a little further, after checking his watch to make sure he had enough time. Going further down, he noticed a strange looking machine on the sidewalk. He was drawn by curiosity to the machine. It turned to be a simple weight machine. Acting on a childish impulse, Robert took out a coin and inserted it in the slot. A card popped out and Robert was stunned to read it. It said: "Good evening, Mr. Smith, you weigh 175 pounds. Hope you enjoy your midnight flight to Los Angeles." How could a simple machine know his name, and his plans?" he thought. Amazing!

Robert was tempted to try checking again, to see if it was all really happening. He went through the procedure of positioning himself correctly and inserting the coin in the slot. The card that came out read, "Good evening, Mr. Smith, you still weigh 175 pounds. Hope you enjoy your midnight flight to Los Angeles." Now Robert was truly taken aback. He still couldn't figure out how a simple machine could tell so much about him. He had to know. It was getting more and more curious. He stood wondering on the various theories and possibilities that could have gone into making the special machine. He mentally worked out many combinations. Nothing seemed convincing. After a while, he decided to test the machine again. This time, he carefully removed his dress shoes and jacket and placed them at a distance from the machine. He then stood on the machine and inserted one of his last coins. The card that came out read, "Good evening, with or without shoes and jacket, you are still Mr. Smith and you still weigh 175 pounds. But, I'm sorry to say that you just missed your midnight flight to Los Angeles."

How many of you can relate to Robert? Distracted by events and people, real or imagined, we lose sight of our immediate goals in life. Distracted, Robert lost sight of his immediate goal which was catching the flight to

Los Angeles and replaced it with one that would be of no benefit to him 15 minutes later. Focus on the destination, not the hurdles between you and it. This is what kept Jeremiah going. He knew that if he didn't change the people's outlook they would all die.

We live in a time when it is easy to show up every day and live a lie. We act all righteous around our coworkers and strangers but live our lives like there is no Hell. You can impress men all day long but God sees what man does not, and he is probably not impressed. It is good to read about a man like Jeremiah who was willing to speak out against the evil in his society and stand up for truth but how many of us are willing to duplicate his actions? How many of us would persevere under such conditions? Jeremiah's perseverance teaches us a lesson that can change peoples lives even today. Even yours.

Chapter 15
Mighty Men Have No Fear

Obi-Wan: I have something here for you. Your father wanted you to have this when you were old enough, but your uncle wouldn't allow it. He feared you might follow old Obi-Wan on some damn fool idealistic crusade like your father did. It's your father's lightsaber. This is the weapon of a Jedi Knight. Not as clumsy or as random as a blaster, but an elegant weapon for a more civilized age. For over a thousand generations, the Jedi Knights were the guardians of peace and justice in the Old Republic. Before the dark times, before the Empire. - Star Wars IV

Fear has been a part of our emotional makeup since the fall of man. When Adam and Eve rebelled against the Lord, they hid themselves from Him and were afraid. Things haven't changed much. Fear affects our thinking and controls our actions. It can and will keep us from moving forward into any uncharted territory we may wish to explore in our lives. Fear is a stifling force that will keep us from reaching our goals, but it can be conquered.

During World War II, General George Patton was met by a military governor who praised his bravery in battle. General Patton replied, "Sir, I am not a brave man – the truth is, I am an utter craven coward. I have never been within the sound of gunshot or in sight of battle in my whole life that I wasn't so scared that I had sweat in the palms of my hands." We ask ourselves, how could such a man function with these fears weighing on him? Many years later Patton wrote in his autobiography, "I learned very early in my life never to take counsel of my fears."

In 333 BC Alexander fell sick after bathing in a cold stream, so his physician and life-long friend Phillip prepared a remedy for him. As he was about to drink he received a letter from one of his generals warning that Phillip might try to poison him. According to the account, Alexander read the letter and while drinking the remedy handed the note to Phillip. Through this act Alexander showed Phillip that he was not afraid and therefore trusted him. His actions told this general that he was steadfast in refusing to suspect his friends.

When faced with a trying situation most people attempt to reason with their fears. You might as why this is...it's because we are logical beings. We tend to move towards things that are reasonable or that have some sort of well-thought out principle. The problem stems from the fact that logic has little to do with emotional experiences. Your subconscious mind can't tell the difference between what is real and what is not. Your mind accepts information without question and then acts on that input. Once it believes something is true, it seeks to make it that way in the real world.

A field full of barley. What an insignificant-seeming thing to defend! Yet Eleazar understood the importance of not giving an inch of his territory to the enemy. Eleazar was one of David's three top mighty men and a descendant of the tribe of Benjamin. It seems that several of his relatives were soldiers in David's army and had made names for themselves because of their courage. He was with David when the Israelites took on the Philistines gathered at Pas Dammim for battle. The men of Israel retreated, but he stood his ground and struck down the Philistines till his hand grew tired and froze to the sword. The men of Israel had deserted him; he could have been killed. Nevertheless, there was no spite in his heart; he held no grudge against them. The troops returned to Eleazar, patted him on the back and began to strip the dead. Eleazar was victorious that day, but what was his secret? Eleazar means "the Lord is my helper." From his very name we learn we cannot fight all the battles on our own. Success in battle comes from allowing God to work through us.

Eleazar represented a different breed of man. A man who would put on his game face to stand and defend what was his, no matter what the cost. Eleazar's determination to win was so great that his hand would not let go of his sword when it was all over, and needed to be pried free. The battles we face will sometimes press us to the point of exhaustion but the results are worth the effort only if we are willing to stay in the fight! The Bible tells us that God worked a great victory through Eleazar because of his perseverance and courage that day. It also tells us that we to can have that same sense of victory if only we have the same courage.

I once watched a documentary on the racing of the Baja 1000 in which one fellow was attempting ride the entire length of the course alone on a motorcycle. Most teams who attempt this race do it with groups of four or more riders in which they switch off and on every hundred miles or so. The Baja 1000 is the longest off-road race in world, so to try to race it by yourself riding a motorcycle the entire way is an interesting challenge. What was so interesting about this particular event was at the very end when this particular rider had finished and won the race, his support team gathered around to congratulate him but in order to do so they had to pry his hands from the handlebars of the bike. His willingness to overcome his fear and press on through whatever challenges that may come his way literally "froze" his hands to the motorcycle. We as Mighty Men need this kind of courage and level of perseverance.

If we want to win this fight then we need courage to defy the enemy and the initiative to try. Eleazar went on the offensive! It takes more courage to say "I'll try" than "I cannot" sometimes it takes individual initiative to see a group succeed. Those who follow the crowd usually do not become leaders, but rather they become followers. The fight cannot be delayed until we have a bigger group to support us or more weapons at our disposal. The enemy will not wait until you think it is a more convenient time. Sometimes we just have to do what we need to with what we have, digging deep for the necessary courage and never giving up.

Eleazar just would not give up. I once heard, "The measure of a man is what it takes to make him quit." The average person would have seen the odds against them and tucked tail. Eleazar wasn't average. He was a Mighty Man of Valor and no one could take that away from him. Not the Philistines. Not his own army, in fact the only person who could take it away from him was himself. To all outward appearances the situation was hopeless, especially in light of the superior might of the Philistines. He could have quit and run in fear, like all of his fellow "warriors." He could have given up out of sheer exhaustion. His hand was frozen to his sword! Instead, Eleazar just kept fighting. Eleazar knew that one man willing to set the example and not give up could overcome any enemy. Courage and initiative can get us into a fight, but it will take even more courage and endurance to get us out.

Galatians 6:9 says "And let us not be weary in well doing: for in due season we shall reap, if we faint not" Eleazar refused to let his fears direct his actions.

Doctors have said that we are only born with two fears, the fear of loud noises and the fear of falling. If this is true then every other fear is created by us and can therefore be overcome and eliminated by us. We are human beings. If we can create it, then we can destroy it. Most of our fears are created by our own experiences such as what someone has told you, or what you read in the papers and watch on the television. I have seen people afraid to drive their cars because they were afraid if they used too much gas they might single-handledly cause a nationwide energy crisis. All because they heard on the news that the price of gas was going up. The price of gas increasing does not mean that there is a shortage of oil in the world. It means that somewhere, someone wants to make more money. It also shows how easily we can create fear within us.

Let me give you an example of how people let their fears direct their actions. In early 2008, my wife and I decided to stop by a local motorcycle dealership and look at a bike. I had been pondering the purchase of one for a while, and besides, I just like hanging out in motorcycle shops. Upon arriving we noticed that there was a large number of people milling around inside. There were more people than one would normally expect on this particular day. I cornered one of the salesmen and asked him what was going on. His response was that since the price of gas had skyrocketed to over four dollars per gallon, more and more people had begun to turn to buying small motorcycles in an effort to curb their spending on gas. I'll be honest, I thought he was joking. I replied to him you mean to tell me that these people are willing to spend three to four thousand dollars to save a few cents on gas? He said it was so bad that the dealership's inventory of pre-ordered vehicles was already sold out and that the only bikes left were the bigger engine models…which by the way get almost the same gas mileage as their smaller counterparts. My first thought centered on how much gas one could buy with four thousand dollars. Lisa and I just shook our heads in amazement and went on to the other errands we had for that day.

A few months later, Lisa and I were looking to purchase a new SUV and had been going from dealership to dealership test driving different vehicles. The first thing we noticed was that the models we were looking at all had some great incentives on them due to the fact that they had larger displacement engines than some other available models. The reason for the incentives was again because of the price of gas. People didn't want to buy an SUV with a big engine for fear that the price of gas would go up again, so the dealerships were offering everything within their power to promote sales on these vehicles. We got a great deal! Two days later, Lisa had to take the SUV back to the dealership to have the remote start installed. On the day we purchased the vehicle the showroom was a ghost town but on this day it was swamped with people. Lisa asked one of the salesmen what was going on. Was there a huge sale going on? Did some new incentives come out? The reason for the large influx of people in the dealership TWO DAYS LATER was that the price of oil had dropped $10 per barrel. The people who were buying mid to large SUVs like these were the last ones on the planet and they were doing it without any of the previous incentives. Some were even paying as much as $3000 over invoice!

All this because people had let their fear of an impending gas shortage or a massive increase in prices affect their decisions. I calculated the incentives that we had been able to take advantage of plus the overage in selling price and came to the conclusion that some of these kind people were paying as much as $8000 more for the same vehicle I purchased two days before. Do you know how much gas one can buy for $8000? Don't get me wrong I am completely on the side of being financially responsible but sometimes we need to sit down and think about the decisions we are making and *why* we are making them.

Fears, even the smaller ones, can completely destroy your dreams. It can destroy fortunes as well as relationships. If unchecked it can wipe out entire lives. Many think that fear is something that you fight against and to some degree this is true but in reality to focus on the fear will only bring more of it of it into your life. Remember, anything that you focus on your mind will work to create more of. If you focus on how bad your financial situation is your mind will create more of the situation, whereas if you focus on how to overcome the situation your mind will create a way.

160

There are other types of fear that we as men must work on each and every day to conquer in our lives.

Doubt

Have you ever had a great idea and almost immediately you began to doubt whether or not you should say anything for fear that you may not be able to pull it off? In a matter of seconds something that was so awesome has been lost because of your own unwillingness to follow it to fruition. People doubt many things such as the government, their church, their spouses, their kids, and worst of all themselves. If you don't overcome your doubt and have faith it will eventually destroy any chance of success and quite possibly your life. Doubt can rob you of your bank account and relieve you of your soul. The best way to overcome doubt is to be willing to take a chance and see what happens. The answer to conquering doubt is belief. Take a moment to look deep down inside and see whether or not you believe. Believe that you will be able to figure out all the solutions and overcome all the challenges. Believe that you will come out on top and be a winner. Here is a big one: believe that you deserve success. Believe that you have the capability to fight against all the odds. I once read a quote that it was better to have tried and failed than to never have tried at all. To never attempt anything will always leave you with the feeling that you may have succeeded if you had only tried.

Indifference

Have you ever said something to a teenager and received the all-encompassing response: "Yeah Whatever?" Translation is: I don't care either way. People don't care about things because they don't think it will affect them or they don't want to get involved. They are really just drifting through life and drifters rarely drift to any specific destination. No one ever drifts to the mountain top so even though you may be afraid of what is on top of the mountain you will never know for sure until you make a point of getting there. When we are indifferent we tell others that what we have to offer is unimportant. We say to ourselves, "They would never be interested in something like this." We have just made an assumption about our offering's perceived value. Just because what we have to offer may be without value to any one particular individual doesn't mean that that there are not other people out there who may appreciate the value.

Take a moment to consider the things that are important to you. Think about the reasons that you believe these things are important. The best way to overcome indifference is to replace it with passion. What is your passion? What is the benefit to you? How could this same passion be of value to someone else? Test your theory by letting go of your "stinking thinking" and ask. Passion is a byproduct of the condition of your heart and it breeds conviction within you. When people are allowed to see your passion they then can decide whether they want to be a part of it.

Indecision

Former president Ronald Reagan once had an aunt who took him to a cobbler for a pair of new shoes. The cobbler asked young Reagan, "Do you want square toes or round toes?" Unable to decide, Reagan didn't answer, so the cobbler gave him a few days. Several days later the cobbler saw Reagan on the street and asked him again what kind of toes he wanted on his shoes. Reagan still couldn't decide, so the shoemaker replied, "Well, come by in a couple of days. Your shoes will be ready." When the future president did so, he found one square-toed and one round-toed shoe! "This will teach you to never let people make decisions for you," the cobbler said to his indecisive customer. "I learned right then and there," Reagan said later, "if you don't make your own decisions, someone else will."

Indecision can and will rob you of opportunity. It can rob you of any chance for a better life if you let it. A person can decide to be decisive by mentally making a point to be quicker at making decisions and slow to change them. Lisa and I have some good friends whom we love dearly and get together with quite often. As with many great friendships this one got started on rocky ground. We used to get together for an evening of board games which at the time used to drive me to the point of insanity. One member of this couple had the hardest time making decisions while playing the games. It wasn't like we were playing a thought-provoking game like Risk or Axis and Allies. We played cards most of the time and this one particular individual used to drag the games out for hours due to their lack of decision making ability. It drove me to the point where I didn't want to get together with them for fear of losing my temper in the middle of the game. This person acted like every decision they made was life or death. It may be funny to you but upon further introspection I

162

realized they weren't the only ones in the world that were this way. Many people cannot make a decision for fear of the outcome.

You'll get better at having patience with these people by realizing that not everyone has the same mindset regarding decision-making that you do. . I realized that these game sessions were great practice for the indecisive, because that person was forced to practice decision-making. It may be babysitting children or volunteering to lead a squad of Marines into a firefight. Either example will put you in situations where decisions must be made now! Once you have overcome the indecision you will be surprised at the number of opportunities that will become available to you.

Worry
It's been said that the average person's anxiety breaks down like this…

* 40%—things that will never happen
* 30%—things about the past that can't be changed
* 12%—things about criticism by others, mostly untrue
* 10%—about health, which gets worse with stress
* 8%—about real problems that will be faced

There are many kinds of worry. You can worry about what people think or do. You can worry about what will happen (or will not happen). You can worry about why you worry so much. Worry is the expectation of an event that may not come to pass. The key to getting worry out of your life lies in your self-confidence and expectations. If you worry too much it's most likely because your expectations are low. If you don't worry enough (is there really such a thing?) then your expectations may be overconfident. You must find a level of balance in your expectations which will therefore help you balance any worries you may have.

Change
Picture a scene from the Old West, sometime in the 1870s. Weary cowboys in dusty Levi's gather around a blazing campfire after a day on the open range. The lonely howl of a coyote counterpoints the notes of a guitar as the moon floats serenely overhead. Suddenly a bellow of pain shatters the night, as a cowpoke leaps away from the fire, dancing in agony. Hot-Rivet Syndrome has claimed another victim. In those days,

Levi's were made, as they had been from the first days of Levi Strauss, with copper rivets at stress points to provide extra strength. On these original Levi's—model 501—the crotch rivet was the critical one: when cowboys crouched too long beside the campfire, the rivet grew uncomfortably hot. For years the brave men of the West suffered this curious occupational hazard. Then, in 1933, Walter Haas, Sr., president of Levi Strauss, went camping in his Levi 501's. He was crouched by a crackling campfire in the High Sierras, drinking in the pure mountain air, when he fell prey to Hot-Rivet Syndrome. He consulted with professional wranglers in his party. Had they suffered the same mishap? An impassioned YES was the reply. Haas vowed that the offending rivet must go, and at their next meeting the board of directors voted it into extinction.
- Everybody's Business, ed. by M. Moskowitz, M. Katz, R. Levering

Everyone fears change at some point until they begin to understand the purpose and benefit of change. Change allows you to become someone different than who you are. It allows you to do something different than you're doing. Some of you are saying, but I like who I am and what I am doing, but that doesn't mean the people around you do. You do remember those people don't you? The ones you're supposed to be leading and serving? They may not like whom they are or what they are doing and need someone to show them a different way. You cannot do that without change.

Failure
After the horrible carnage and Confederate retreat at Gettysburg, General Robert E. Lee wrote this to Jefferson Davis, president of the Confederacy:

> *"We must expect reverses, even defeats. They are sent to teach us wisdom and prudence, to call forth greater energies, and to prevent our falling into greater disasters."*

The only person who avoids failure is the one who never leaves his house and that in itself is a failure. Look at it this way, if we decide that there is no failure but rather just opportunities to learn and try again, doesn't that make failing much less awe inspiring? When you have the right attitude failure is neither fatal nor final. I once heard a military slogan that stated Try, Fail, and Adjust. I prefer to modify it a bit to Try, Learn, and Adjust.

If we try and do not succeed then we are given a chance to learn and adjust whatever needs adjusting, after which we can try again. Applying this thought process to any challenging situation will allow you the opportunity to succeed where others may have failed before. It's OK to not succeed at everything as long as you don't consider yourself a failure. The only way one truly fails is if they give up.

We all face obstacles in life and most of them are self imposed. It is only natural to be afraid when facing an unknown situation but what isn't natural is letting it control you. Rather than waiting for fear to go away, be a man and take steps to overcome the situation. Identify the pay-offs for each decision and discover what is keeping you from taking action. Once identified, you can then make changes which will increase your sense of worth. Whatever you do, don't play the blame game. It is very easy to put yourself in a position where all forward motion has stopped because you want to justify the reason as being something or someone else. Benjamin Franklin, author, diplomat, inventor, physicist, politician, & printer said, *"Do not anticipate trouble, or worry about what may never happen. Keep in the sunlight"*.

Men must continue to persevere in the battle to overcome their fears. It is not a battle of swords, or even tanks and guns. It takes place on the battlefield of our hearts and minds but it can be easy for that battle to spill over into our physical world and there will be times when we may be called upon to suffer for that fear. I pray that each of you may do so with courage.

Chapter 16
Might Men are Consistent

The unfortunate thing about this world is that good habits are so much easier to give up than bad ones. ~Somerset Maugham

Think about your day. A typical day might look something like this: Wake up, hop in the shower, brush your teeth, comb your hair, get some coffee and a bowl of Honey Nut Cheerios (my favorite), then out the door to work. All of these activities show that you are consistent in your life. You do them day after day, week after week, year after year with very little variation. You are consistent but sometimes you wonder if any of it matters. I am here to tell you that everything you do matters! People form habits, and habits form futures. Let's take brushing your teeth for example. You probably brush your teeth twice a day. What if you don't? Well, you would have bad breath, yellow teeth and eventually your teeth would fall of out your head from rot. So we brush them daily to ensure their longevity and cleanliness.

Think of what you could accomplish if you could apply that same consistency to all your habits. We all have habits, some of them are good and others are bad. Many are productive and more are not. They have been defined as unconscious patterns of behavior. We have bathing habits, grooming habits, eating habits, exercise habits, work habits, play habits, love habits, hate habits, study habits, sleeping habits, waking habits, conscious habits, unconscious habits, habits we only have when we are by ourselves and habits when we are in company. We have habits that other people are attracted to and others that repel. Many people love us for our habits and hate us for the same. Most of life is habitual. You do the same things you did yesterday, the day before, and every day for the last month. To some degree, habits make us who we are. The key is learning how to control them so that they do not control us. If you can learn to change your habits you can change your life. So let's examine our habits, both good and bad, and see where we need to go with that knowledge.

The Bad [Habits Mighty Men Must Avoid]:

Inconsistency

If you have ever played golf you know important consistency is. To achieve any sort of goal, the golfer needs a swing that is repeatable under pressure every time they play. Developing that swing, however, isn't easy. It takes hard work and plenty of practice. The ideal scenario involves you starting by taking short swings such as a putt and moving up to longer swings until you eventually master the drive. Leadership consistency is the same way. We must learn to master the little things before we can expect to tackle the larger ones. We as Mighty Men must strive to be consistent in our behavioral responses, expectations, and judgment. Those whom we lead, whether they are an organization or our families, are looking for consistency in our lives. They want to see that we act and react the same during the good times and the bad. They want to know that we have the ability to stay the course, demonstrating confidence and control in all we do.

During World War II, Major Dick Winters commanded Easy Company, 2nd Battalion, 506th Parachute Infantry Regiment, 101st Airborne Division. While his unit was stationed at the marshaling area in Devon, England, Major Winters had to discipline a fellow officer and friend. Lieutenant Lynn 'Buck' Compton had developed the habit of gambling with the men under his command. This put him in the embarrassing position of taking from those he led if he won. Major Winter's point in disciplining Lt. Compton was that a person must always find ways to give to those they lead, not take from them. He believed you must give in every way; you must give of your time and energy. You must be consistent in your treatment of them. You must never show them how to do something and then you yourself do it differently.

Let me ask you this; do you act differently when you're out with your friends than when you're out with your family? Are you consistent in your actions no matter where you are or who you are with? In order to be an effective influence on those around us, we must learn to be consistent in our actions, convictions, and attitudes. Inconsistent behavior is one of the fastest ways for anyone to lose the trust we work so hard to earn. Trust is built through a succession of consistent behaviors. Whether you are trying out a new workout regimen or a parenting technique, you will find that by developing a certain level of consistency, the task will become easier as time progresses. Improvement at any task or of any skill is impossible without consistent effort.

However, there are times and situations where inconsistency can be a positive attribute; trying something new can be healthy and may even lead to a new good habit. Instead of getting up at 6:05 every Saturday morning, just like you would on a weekday, sleep until 8:00; instead of working through your lunch hour, go for a walk; find a new way to drive to work; switch chores with your spouse; take up a hobby that interests someone else; stay up till 3:00am playing board games with your friends; visit some veterans at the local assisted living facility; subscribe to a new magazine; go white-water rafting; learn to speak a new language; teach someone the thing you do best; take up ballroom dancing; remember, we pass this way only once.

Criticism
Have you ever been criticized by someone? Do you remember how you felt? It wasn't that great of a feeling was it? Have you ever wondered why people feel the need to do that? Anytime you try to make your mark in this life, you will attract people who want to erase that mark. People criticize because they feel inadequate and they want to feel superior to other people. Their self-esteem is so low they usually put other people down through criticism so they can feel better about themselves. If you think about it, they really are not putting you down as much as they are depreciating their own worth. Their criticism does lower our self-esteem somewhat, if we choose to let it, but not as much as it lowers theirs. Elizabeth Harrison, daughter of President Benjamin Harrison, is quoted as saying "Those who are lifting the world upward and onward are those who encourage more than criticize."

My first gut reaction to criticism is to return the favor with my own criticism, but I have found this is a good way to start a fight that no one really wins. The best way, I have found, to combat criticism is to ask questions to try to find out why they are saying these things. Learn to put them on the defensive but don't do it by attacking them. By making the other person defend themselves you will find that there is most likely a

168

challenge in their life that is manifesting itself outwardly through their criticism. Acknowledge a person's strengths and accomplishments before plunging into recognizing their weaknesses. Build them up as a person first before pointing out their flaws. By becoming aware of other people's problems we become capable of stopping the habit in ourselves and then we are able to handle it. When we realize that the criticism is coming from people who are in pain and have no other way to handle it, we ourselves become more capable of dealing with it. Remember this next time someone is overly critical of you.

Did you know that refusing to listen is a form of criticism? People don't like to talk for talking's sake. They like to know that what they are saying is being received, processed, analyzed, and acted upon even if it just looks like it's being considered. When people know that you're not listening it makes them give up trying to communicate, which stagnates any positive constructive environment you may have been trying to create.

> *"Flatter me and I may not believe you. Criticize me and I may not like you. Ignore me and I may not forgive you. Encourage me and I will not forget you"* - William Arthur Ford

Overprotection
We as men have been tasked with the duty of protector of all that is our responsibility. Sometimes we take it a little too far though. We think that the best way to protect those we love is to bury them in rules and regulations. We have strict rules about everything; where to be, when to be, how to be, what to be. The danger in this is that we develop a controlling mindset which we think gives us license to own or dominate. We figure that if our charges never break the rules then they cannot get themselves into any trouble. The danger in never allowing them their liberty is that they never learn to make decisions for themselves. They eventually lose trust in us and themselves. I am not saying that you should not have any rules but we need to analyze the rules we do have and make sure they do not stifle creativity. We want our people to be creative because creative people do not focus on limitations, but rather focus on the possibilities.

I heard an illustration once that I thought was a great example of how we as Mighty Men must learn the place of rules. Have you ever stood in the shower and tried to grasp the wet bar of soap? If you grab it too hard it pops right out of your hand but if you don't grab it hard enough it slips out of your hand and onto the floor. The way we deal with rules must be the same way. There must be a balance in the way we mete out the rules. Too hard and they will rebel against us, too soft and they will slip every time.

Irritability

Irritability is a negative outward manifestation of your current state of mind. It tells people that you're not completely in control of your emotions and therefore cannot be trusted with any actions. You may tend to leap to conclusions and misinterpret the intentions of others. You may feel that you are too easily taken advantage of and more likely to become angry. Irritability is a term for the emotional tone that usually precedes anger. You can do many things with anger. You can repress it, act out on it, or you can control it and use it to some productive purpose. Besides, people just don't want to be around irritable people. They feel that it brings them down and most people realize they are perfectly capable of doing that themselves and do not need anyone else's help. If people don't want to be around you then you most likely will not be in a position to influence them. If you don't influence people they cannot learn to trust you and if they don't trust you, your role will be seriously compromised. Maybe you have just quit smoking and the cravings are driving you crazy or you just started a new diet and the thought of Krispy Kreme donuts is really driving you insane. Either case is a prime example of why we must control our emotions. If we let them run rampant we cannot and will not achieve our goal of losing weight or saying goodbye to our nicotine addiction.

Favoritism

Favoritism refers to when someone appears to be treated better than you for no valid reason. This can create a level of frustration that is very hard to step back from. Forget about being objective! Maybe our coworker who does less work than us just got the bigger office or possibly it's a sibling who never seems to do anything wrong. These are all forms of favoritism, if we choose to see them that way. If all of us were to be honest, most would admit to having favorites but that doesn't mean we have to display favoritism. Put two or more children in one family and someone will eventually cry "you treat them better than me!" So that leads to the question of the validity of the complaint. Because they are different people with different personalities you will, by definition, treat them differently. The bottom line is this: Even if you do treat your children differently, this presents you as the parent with a prime opportunity to teach your children how to manage themselves in situations that might be unfair. It's great training for the real world and also tells them that one doesn't not lower their standards of behavior just because "you treat them differently than me!"

The Good [Habits Mighty Men Must Adopt]:

Standards
Leading people and setting the standards by which an organization is run by is not all that difficult as long as one is consistent with those standards. Organizations, whether a business or a family, should be run by the leader and not by the people being led. So many times, however, the followers find themselves in charge because the leader is so eager to be liked, and whatever rules and standards that were established are rarely enforced. It is up to you as the head of your family to define what is acceptable and what is not. When we give consistent messages concerning dangerous and unacceptable behavior, it will be easier for those we lead to forego the temptation of participation. It is our responsibility as leaders to help them learn that actions have consequences. It is our responsibility to instruct them when they have overstepped a behavioral boundary. Those whom we help to develop a habit of setting standards for their lives will always be in positions of strength and their choices will be become clearer because they have been given a framework to guide their decision-making processes. Because they now have a baseline to refer to, they will be much less apt to lower the standards of their lives just so their friends who lack commitment will feel accommodated.

Communication Skills
Learning to communicate with people, not only on a verbal level, but also on an emotional one will propel you much further in reaching your goals than you will ever imagine possible. If you think about it, right now every aspect of your appearance and habits has an effect on your

communications skills. Everything from the way you dress to the way you comb your hair communicates to those around you what you're thinking and doing. Let's start with the inside and work our way out to see what I mean.

Check your attitude. People are attracted to those who have a positive outlook and perspective. Make a conscious decision to be upbeat and optimistic and leave the doom and gloom to others. By doing this you will find yourself standing above the crowd! Ask yourself, why am I here? What do I hope to gain or accomplish? What do I have to offer this person? Your positive mental preparation will eventually be transmitted outward through your speech, so if you're thinking negative thoughts guess what the other person will hear?

Dress appropriately. Everything from your hair to your shoes is an indicator of who you are, and what your purpose might be. The image you project gives people a first impression of your character. Haven't we all heard, "You never get a second chance to make a first impression?" Many times I see teenagers showing up on interviews wearing the same clothes that they might wear to the mall with their friends. Young people need to realize or be taught that they are not trying to impress their friends but rather someone who wants to know if they would be a good addition to their organization. I hear the argument all the time that "I don't want to impress them with my clothes. I want them to be impressed with my work ethic." That's great but they have no idea what your work ethic is and are most likely not going to get a chance to figure out if they are scared by how you look. I am not saying we all have to dress like our parents but maybe a little research might be in order. Find out what kind of person the interviewee is and how they themselves might dress, you can then dress accordingly.

Smile. It has been said that people who smile are 100 times more attractive than people who don't. Doctors tell us that it takes more muscles to frown than it takes to smile, so smiling is easier. Smiling once in a while lets people know that you are friendly, which breeds likeability and then trust. People prefer to do business with and ally themselves with people they like and trust.

Have a firm handshake. Most men cannot stand someone with a weak handshake. It's a sign of a weak person and no one wants to be around weak people. If your handshake is like a dead fish on the end of your arm, you are telling the other person that you are not interested in meeting them. On the opposite side, you don't need to have a bone-crushing, "bring 'em to their knees" shake either. Make it firm. The strength of your handshake will project your self-image and confidence to others.

Make eye contact. You take in stimuli through every one of your senses such as your ears and touch but your eyes are the only sense mechanism that connects directly to your brain. Look the person you're speaking to in the eye and think to yourself: "You're a great person." Your positive thoughts will be communicated through your eyes. Talk with your eyes. Listen with your eyes. Developing the habit of looking someone in the eye as you speak to them is a tell-tale sign of your own self-respect, and an outward sign of your respect for the other person. Keep this in mind: The eyes are the window to the soul; will people like what they see?

Listen. We were all born with two ears and one mouth. The challenge is that we tend to use them disproportionately. We use our mouthes more than we use our ears. Learn to be sincere and reduce the "I" in your speech patterns. Replace it with "you" and people will tell you everything you ever wanted to know.

Refusing to rest on your laurels
In the Greek games of the ancient world, the winner of an event was crowned with a laurel wreath. But the winner could not "rest on his laurels" if he wanted to remain a champion. Everyone learns this truth from experience. A quick way to go downhill from the peak of performance is to stop training when the race is over and rely on past accomplishments. For some, as sometimes happens with winners of gold medals in modern Olympic Games, the award is enough. It means that they have reached the top and no longer need to climb any higher. You as a leader can never let yourself fall into this trap. To get to this point means that you have told yourself there are no more mountains to conquer and nothing left to learn. Basking in the glories of past victories can lead to future defeat because our battles never stop and neither do the battles of the people we lead. There will always be something you don't know and

someone who needs your help. Take the time and energy to invest in yourself and keep learning. New strategies and new ideas are always being implemented which means if you want to stay current then you need to keep up. Technology and the world in general are always changing so if we don't keep our eye on it we can be left behind.

Developing your mind
Your mind is the best weapon in your arsenal but, much like all tools, requires constant maintenance and care. As technology advances, we as individuals have become increasingly dependent on the computer and other modern conveniences. What happens if the electricity goes off? What happens when your car doesn't start? Do you know how to entertain your kids when the Playstation or the Wii breaks? Do not be so reliant on technology that you forget to use good, old-fashioned common sense. Read more. Study more. Life itself can be the best teacher but will only instruct you in the subjects you are willing to learn. Barring some unforeseen mental challenge, you possess all the elements needed for success in any arena. Scientists have said for years that we only use, at most, ten percent of our available mental capacity. Some of us don't even use that much. You can never hope to expand the capacity of your mind until you learn to control it. You have to direct and discipline its activity. You must learn to control your reactions to things and then use these stimuli to fuel our behaviors. As you learn and experience things, you will develop an understanding of yourself and others that will become very profitable in many areas of your life.

When we are old and gray and all our good looks have gone south for the winter of our lives or when we have done as much as possible and the work before us is done, all that will remain is who we are. Your position as a Mighty Man of Valor will not be judged by what pinnacle you reached in this life but rather by the obstacles you overcame while in that situation and the habits you kept. When all is said and done more will be said by our habits and the legacy they leave behind.

Chapter 17
Lessons from the Field

Yours is the profession of arms, the will to win, the sure knowledge that in war there is no substitute for victory, that if you lose, the Nation will be destroyed, that the very obsession of your public service must be Duty, Honor, Country. - General Douglas MacArthur's Farewell Speech. Given to the Corps of Cadets at West Point May 12, 1962

Samson, a member of the tribe of Dan, was one of the Judges of Israel, a title he held for 20 years. Before he was born, Samson's mother was barren but received a visit from an angel one night, who told her she would give birth to an unusual son, and to not cut his hair. This angel obviously never visited my mother! Samson was endowed with great strength which he used to kill a lion with his bare hands, and later ended the existence of 1,000 Philistines with the jawbone of a donkey. He also had his share of romantic encounters with three different women. One of the women, Delilah, not only caught his eye but his heart as well. Everything was going fine until his enemies decided to coerce Delilah into being a spy for them. They wanted to know Samson's secret, what made him so strong, so they could subdue him. She eventually nagged him enough and found out it was because his hair had never been cut. So Samson goes to sleep, they cut his hair off, he loses his strength, end of story right? With his strength gone he was easily captured by the Philistines, who gouged out his eyes, and made him grind grain in their prison.

Later, the Philistines made a spectacle of Samson in the center of a temple during a celebration. One small problem though, his hair had now grown back and some moron thought it would be a good idea to place the worlds strongest man between two support columns. Samson asked God to strengthen him one last time "so that I may pay back the Philistines for the loss of at least one of my eyes." Then Samson pushed against the pillars with all his might and the temple came crashing down, taking out more Philistines than Samson had killed during his entire lifetime. Samson died in the ensuing collapse and his brothers recovered his body and brought him home to be buried with his parents. What's to learn here? I am getting to that, so just be patient.

After graduating from the United States Military Academy in 1898, and serving with the Cuban occupation force, Fox Connor developed a reputation as a rising star in the pre-World War I Army. He served on the Army General Staff, as an instructor at the War College, and in several other positions in which he influenced the future direction of the Army. During World War I, Conner was tapped by General John J. Pershing to be the chief of operations (three stars? G3) for the American Expeditionary Force in France. For his service as the "brain" of the AEF, Conner was awarded a number of medals; and after the war, he wrote an after-action report that influenced the 1920 National Defense Act which set the course of the Army between the world wars.

Conner's most-lasting contribution, though, was his mentorship of a young Army officer named Dwight Eisenhower. They first met when Eisenhower was stationed at the Infantry Tank School at Camp Meade in 1919. The two men immediately developed a great mutual respect so great that when Conner took command of the 20th Infantry Brigade in Panama, he invited Eisenhower to join his staff. For three years, Conner instituted a systematic course of study for Eisenhower that ranged from extensive readings in military history to daily practical experience writing field orders for every aspect of the command. Finally, Conner pulled strings to get his protégé admitted to the Command and Staff School, where Eisenhower graduated first in his class, thanks in no small part to the comprehensive tutelage from Conner early in his career.

Eisenhower learned much from Conner, about leadership and the conduct of war. Conner had three principles of war that he imparted to Eisenhower which we will use as guidelines for conducting day to day operations as a mighty man of valor. We will also learn how Samson applied these principals almost three thousand years before Fox Connor. Conner's Three Principles:

Never fight unless you have to.
From the moment we all wake up in the morning we will be presented with choices as to whether we will get into the fight or not. The question will always be do we fight? Either you face the challenge and fight or run away with your tail between your legs. Maybe your neighbor ran over your garbage can on his way to work, or maybe your teenage daughter just

showed up at the breakfast table wearing less-than-appropriate clothing. In each situation you will have the opportunity to decide whether it's worth fighting for or maybe you should capitulate. Experience will teach you that some threats can be overcome diplomatically while others must be met head on with weapons drawn. Whichever path you choose, engagement without confidence is foolish. If you're cornered and the situation leaves you no choice, prepare yourself mentally and physically and then proceed.

When Samson and his father were on their way to see about getting his first wife and found themselves face to face with the lion, there were really only two choices: (you didn't tell this story about the first wife and the lion) Either to fight or to flee. Fleeing would not have made a very good impression on the young lady who had stolen Samson's heart, so he decided fighting was the better option. Did he have to? Yes, he did! If he didn't do something there was a very good chance the lion would have attacked his future wife-to-be and no mighty man of valor worth his salt can allow that to happen. Our wives are a gift from God and therefore we have been tasked with the responsibility of their protection. To stand idly by and let some danger set upon our wives or our families when we could have done something to prevent it is unconscionable.

Martial Arts style are sometimes categorized into 'hard' and 'soft' disciplines depending on the particular striking and blocking style utilized. A soft style focuses on redirecting your opponent's energy, to throw off balance or move into a better position. Soft styles teach moves that require little energy and are easy to recover from or regain balance if they're blocked. Hard fighting styles, on the other hand, are centered more on offensive moves. The striking techniques in hard styles deliver a lot of power, meaning that a person can be knocked off-balance very easily.

If you do have to fight, a decision must be made as whether to take the hard line or the soft. Will you order your daughter back up to her bedroom to change her clothes or will you explain to her why her choices matter even when it comes to clothes? Will you find out why your neighbor ran over your garbage can or will you find his and destroy it as retribution for the loss of yours? Each choice has far reaching potential but each also goes way beyond the scope of the original problem. Every time you are presented with a confrontational challenge a decision must be made, fight or flee.

Never fight alone.
I once started a business and one of the first principles I learned was that even though I was in business for myself, I wasn't in business by myself. I had people who were willing to help me, but only if I allowed them to. This same promise can be made to people suffering under some sort of addiction. We as men are prone to all kinds of evils that prey upon us each and every day. We fall prey to all manner of sins such as pornography and alcoholism which rob of us of our relationship with the Supreme Commander.

Pornography has been a bane to man's existence since the beginning of time and we will probably have to guard ourselves against it until the very end. Pornography is the coward's solution to a man's constant sexual thoughts. As a man, if you and your wife are having some sort of sexual tension or complete lack of activity, viewing someone else engaged in the act will not provide you with a solution. It will only draw you further and further away from finding an answer together. The Lord has banned such practices in his Army and we know if we are caught that we will have to face a literal spiritual court martial before his throne when our term of enlistment is up in this life.

In Isaiah's time there were men renowned for their drinking. They were no different than those today who boast they can drink anyone under the table. You know who I am talking about. They think it's cool to survive a weekend binge drinking contest. Sometimes they even get to the point where regular alcohol is not enough and they mix in drugs to increase the alcoholic potency. What strength! "I can fry my brain and ruin my body longer than you can!" The sad part is that there are people right now who look up to someone like that as an example. Do you realize how pathetic your own life has to be that a life like that is a step up?

We think we are the only ones who have ever experienced this sort of thing and therefore no one can help us overcome it. Know this though: Other men and women have walked in your shoes and spent sleepless nights trying to work up the courage to stop whatever is tearing them apart

179

or causing their mental and spiritual instability. A good friend will never condemn you for your addiction but don't expect them to support you in continuing in it either. A friend will confront you with the problem and then be ready to help you do whatever is necessary to get you through the pain. The first stop in overcoming an addiction is to stop telling yourself you're faith isn't strong enough. You are an officer in the army of the God of the Universe. He has the power even if you do not. You need to stop blaming it on your parents, your spouse, even your friends. The problem is with you but it is not yours alone. By allowing someone to fight alongside you, you will find you can identify with their own passage through a similar addiction and how they found that path that leads to the other side. You aren't alone. There are others who have taken the same path you're on. They feel as you feel, fight the same shadows as you do, and win or lose just like you.

Some might be reading this right now and asking, "give me one instance where Samson fought with the help of others" to which I will answer; every time he took the field he had help. When he fought the lions he had help. When he mowed down the Philistines he had help and on the day of his resurrection and salvation he had help. He had God's help! And so do you! Samson's strength came directly from God. Without God's help, Samson would not have accomplished one single challenge he ever faced. He would have just been another long haired hippie freak. The great thing is that we as Mighty Men of Valor have that same strength at our disposal. It may not manifest itself in the same manner as it did Samson but if God is with us then nothing is impossible to us. We can do anything, overcome any challenge or solve any problem if we only allow God to work through us. We never ever have to fight alone!

Never fight for long.
This is sound advice for people who are prone to tire from long campaigns. Mighty Men do not tire, though. To become tired means one of two things: Either we are close to victory or we are one step away from giving up or giving in. Some challenges will require more from us than we originally anticipated, but that doesn't mean we must surrender. We must press on but we must also evaluate the reason for the fight and make sure it will move us further towards our eventual goal.
Do you realize that when Samson killed the 1,000 Philistines there were a

lot more around? He could have killed a lot more but only did so to prove a point. He didn't need to kill all of them, only some so that the rest would know that they had no chance of contending with him. This same principle can be applied to our own lives. We don't need to fight every time an opportunity arises, but should only fight those times when the result is the most effective. I was always taught that you should never argue about politics and religion. Later on in life I realized that these were the only two subjects worth arguing about because they are the only two subjects that have any lasting impact. I will debate a person on subjects that deal with a candidate's religious beliefs or their political stand on the issues but I will not argue about anything else. By attacking or defending on those two platforms all the other issues fall into place. Everything about a candidate should come back to one of those two categories. I do this because if I can convince someone that these two positions should line up with their own priorities then all the other issues become unimportant.

Ephesians 4:26 tells us to "Let not the sun go down on your wrath" this basically means not to hold on to your anger for more than one day. Let's say you and your spouse are on a budget and you find out that she went and used the credit card to buy a new dress. If you're like me then you would think this would be a great time to get angry and bring the wrath of Heaven and Earth down on her. STOP! Think for a minute. Is it possible that there was a reason for her violating the agreement of attempting to watch your collective spending? If you cannot discover a viable answer then let her know in a strong tone [not an angry one] that you consider her actions to not be in the best interest of the original plan. Find a way to do it that lets her know that you love her but that you are confused by her decision. Find a solution that both of you can live with and then move on. Don't stew on it for days on end and don't keep reminding her of the choices she has made. These are the kinds of fights that if carried on for too long, you will not win.

Conclusion

"All ammunition expended, bayonet fixed and bloody, one hundred enemy dead all around me, my arms and weapon stretched forward into battle, and my last breath shouting, Attack! Attack! Attack!" - Anonymous soldier when asked what do you want your last words to be? [You The Warrior Leader, Bobby Welch]

If it is your sincere desire to become a Mighty Man of Valor then know this: The opposition will always appear to be greater than your strength until you take that one step forward, make that one decision, or change that one attitude that will allow you to overcome. This will be your defining moment. As Vernon Barr once put it, *"Life is not a journey to the grave with the intention of arriving safely in a pretty and well-preserved body, but rather to skid in broadside, thoroughly used up, totally worn out, and loudly proclaiming: Wow - what a ride!"* Your life right now is your Basic Training. It is your Boot Camp. You are being trained to fight and win but the real ultimate battle will not come until we are long gone from this life. When it is all said and done, your ability as a leader will not be judged by what you have achieved personally or even by what your organization accomplished during your tenure. You will be judged by how well *they* did after you are gone. God is preparing you for enlistment in Heaven's Army and the challenges we face in this life are preparation for that which we will face after graduation.

There will come a day when all Mighty Men of Valor will fight no more. There will be no more battles and no more wars. We will place our weapons and our shields back on the racks in the armory and lock the doors behind us. Many of our friends who have gone on before us will assemble in the Hall of the King to help us celebrate. This will be our Graduation and Retirement Day all in one. There will be no more causes, no more challenges, no more battles, no more criticisms and nothing left to teach. We as Mighty Men know that not all our rewards will be given in this life. All the medals and recognition we may have received in this life will no longer be of any value. We will stand before the Supreme Commander-in-Chief and his generals where he will bestow upon us the greatest award any of us could hope to earn; the "Good and Faithful

182

Servant" medal. It's the highest award for valor in action against an enemy force that can be bestowed upon an individual serving in the Lord's Army. Along with the medal comes a retirement package that is literally out of this world. It is my sincere desire that each and every person who has read this book has gained at least some insight into to what it means to be a Mighty Man of Valor, and more importantly, has learned something that will propel him forward toward becoming the man that he needs to be.

Butch Montgomery
Culpeper, VA

IF

If you can keep your head when all about you
Are losing theirs and blaming it on you,
If you can trust yourself when all men doubt you
But make allowance for their doubting too,
If you can wait and not be tired by waiting,
Or being lied about, don't deal in lies,
Or being hated, don't give way to hating,
And yet don't look too good, nor talk too wise:

If you can dream--and not make dreams your master,
If you can think--and not make thoughts your aim;
If you can meet with Triumph and Disaster
And treat those two impostors just the same;
If you can bear to hear the truth you've spoken
Twisted by knaves to make a trap for fools,
Or watch the things you gave your life to, broken,
And stoop and build 'em up with worn-out tools:

If you can make one heap of all your winnings
And risk it all on one turn of pitch-and-toss,
And lose, and start again at your beginnings
And never breath a word about your loss;
If you can force your heart and nerve and sinew
To serve your turn long after they are gone,
And so hold on when there is nothing in you
Except the Will which says to them: "Hold on!"

If you can talk with crowds and keep your virtue,
Or walk with kings--nor lose the common touch,
If neither foes nor loving friends can hurt you;
If all men count with you, but none too much,
If you can fill the unforgiving minute
With sixty seconds' worth of distance run,
Yours is the Earth and everything that's in it,
And--which is more--you'll be a Man, my son!
Rudyard Kipling

About the Author

Willard "Butch" Montgomery is first and foremost, just a man, who feels the need, deep down, to be something more than he is. He was born and raised in southern Idaho. He has had the honor and privilege of serving in the United States Army Reserve where during his service he was promoted to Specialist and worked as a truck driver, draftsman and combat engineer. Along the way he worked as a architectural designer as well as a construction laborer. He is an Eagle Scout and now runs his own successful web-based marketing company.

Butch doesn't claim to be an expert at anything but that he has learned a thing or two along the path of life. He has been married to his best friend and the love of his life, Lisa, for over 20 years and divides his time between her [she is an author as well] and his three crazy dogs living just outside Washington DC.

www.ingramcontent.com/pod-product-compliance
Lightning Source LLC
Chambersburg PA
CBHW060553200326
41521CB00007B/561